BYRNE'S TREASURY OF
Trick Shots
in Pool
and Billiards

BYRNE'S TREASURY OF
Trick Shots
in Pool
and Billiards

Robert Byrne

A Harvest/HBJ Book
Harcourt Brace Jovanovich, Publishers
San Diego   New York   London

Requests for permission to make copies of any part of the work
should be mailed to:
Permissions Department, Harcourt Brace Jovanovich, Publishers,
Orlando, Florida 32887.

Library of Congress Cataloging in Publication Data

Byrne, Robert, 1930–
Byrne's Treasury of trick shots in pool and billiards.

Bibliography: p.
1. Pool (Game) 2. Billiards. I. Title.
II. Title: Treasury of trick shots in pool and billiards.
III. Title: Trick shots in pool and billiards.
GV891.B964   794.7′3   82-47676
ISBN 0-15-115224-1   AACR2

Printed in the United States of America
First Harvest/HBJ edition 1982

E F G H I

To my many friends in the game
—especially those I didn't mention—
I dedicate this book.

Acknowledgments

Most of the contributors to this book are mentioned at the appropriate places in the text. I owe a special debt of gratitude to Lee Simon, owner of Novato Billiards, for the use and abuse of his equipment; Terry Moldenhauer of Golden West Billiard Mfg. Co. for lending me his remarkable collection of movie stills; Bob Jewett, who has taught me so much about the technicalities of the game; Paul Gerni for giving me the run of his home as well as his notebooks; Jess Meshanic for much valuable historical information and for putting me in touch with wise men from the East; Mike Massey, owner of pooldom's most awesome stroke, for freely sharing his extensive knowledge of trick shots; Jimmy Caras, Ivor Bransford, and Myron Zownir for helpful and stimulating exchanges of letters; Paul Lucchesi, Sr., for helping me push back the origins of many standard shots; Joan Byrne for research at the Library of Congress, Hugh Fraser for research in London, and Joan and Pete Margo for general research assistance; Edward Meyers, Archivist of Ripley International, Ltd., for his thoroughness in searching through the late cartoonist's legacy; Herb Juliano, Curator of the Sports and Games Research Collection at the University of Notre Dame, for furnishing the Mingaud title page; Clem Trainer for unwavering interest and support; Dick Meyers of Billiard Archives for digging up some rare items; Mark Mikulich for the beautiful line drawings of tables, players, and hands; Bill Marshall, also known as Willie Jopling, the world's leading creator of pool trick shots, for an endless stream of information; the staff of Paragraphics for helpfulness and good humor; the late Charlie Peterson, America's greatest exhibition player, for getting me interested in the subject in the first place; and Knox Burger and Kitty Sprague for transcending their roles.

Contents

Book One
POOL

1. Ten Classic Shots 3

2. Ten Classic Variations 15

3. Wisdom of the Ancients 25

4. Twenty-five Easy Ones   41

5. Almost as Easy   59

6. Stymies, Puzzles, and Clusters   73

7. Novelty Shots   87

8.   Tube Shots   101

9.   Shots with One Ball   111

10.   Jump Shots   123

11.   Choice Inner Secrets   137

12. Personal Favorites 155

13. The Great and the Near Great 169

14. Stroke Shots 183

15. Hot Lips and Magic Fingers 195

Book Two
BILLIARDS

3.   Kiss Shots   245

4.   Jump Shots   255

5.   Draw Shots   263

6.   Follow Shots   271

7.   Massé Shots   283

Introduction

This is a book celebrating the recreational aspects of one of the world's oldest and most popular games. The words "trick shots" in the title are taken to mean anything amusing, surprising, educational, or profitable that can be done on a pool or billiard table with standard accessories. Here you'll find shots that require little more than a piece of secret information; spectacular stunts that take years of practice; and novelty items with chalk, coin wrappers, and bottles of beer. For some of the shots you'll need your mouth, your fingers, or your feet.

Trick shots display human creativity at its most beguiling. Some look tough but are so easy they can be made by the clumsiest of television sportscasters; others are so difficult even world champions try them only in private or for each other. As challenges or proposition bets, many trick shots can be used to win money from people you are larger than. While the emphasis is on entertainment, there is plenty here for students as well, for trick shots teach the principles of the game in a vivid and memorable manner. In matches between players of equal skill, victory usually goes to the one who knows the most.

Even though this collection of trick and skill shots is five times bigger than anything similar ever published, it comes nowhere near scraping the bottom of the barrel. The barrel, in fact, is bottomless. Not only is the subject vast and diverse, it's growing, limited solely by the powers of imagination. If I hadn't confined myself to what in my view was the cream of the crop, I could have made nearly every chapter twice as long. New shots are being invented all the time, and in these pages you'll find dozens that were dreamed up during the year the book was in production. More than half of the 350 shots I've chosen to diagram will be new to all but the best-informed professionals. A hundred have never been published anywhere.

In gathering material, I found books published in the nineteenth century to be a rich source, particularly those by Mingaud (1830), Phelan (1858), McCleery (1890), and Thatcher (1898). Present-century books I scavenged include those by Herrmann (1902, reissued in 1967 by Dover), Caras (1948), Ponzi (1948), and Mosconi (1965). A veritable gold mine was an anonymous book called *Trick and Fancy Pocket Billiard Shots,* published in 1918. Only the titles by Herrmann, Caras, and Mosconi are in print and readily available today; among them they describe some 156 shots (with many duplications). From that stock I have chosen only a dozen or two of the best—in almost every case tracing them to earlier writers—preferring to stress less familiar material.

Other printed sources I have drawn upon include the monthly *National Billiard News* (1962–), the bi-monthly *Billiards Digest* (1978–), and the now-defunct *American Billiard Review* (1969–1977). For more details on sources, see the Bibliography on pages 291-292.

Whenever possible, I have named the inventor of the shots described, though seldom with confidence. Even the shots I invented myself may be unconscious borrowings or rediscoveries. The so-called Shoot-off-your-mouth shot, for example, I believe was invented independently by three different players, as detailed on page 14. Because I did not have the assistance of the FBI and the CIA, I was unable to track down the origins of every shot and sort out conflicting claims of authorship. In many cases, the best I could do was tell who showed me the shot. I hope that readers familiar with the literature of pool and billiards will find the attempt to give credit where it is due a refreshing change.

The antiquity of some trick shots is amazing. E. A. White, whose 1807 book was the first in English on the technique of the game, mentions an Italian who was hanging around Paris at the time of the French Revolution in 1789. His specialty was bank shots, and he was willing to bet he could make thirty in a row, not bad considering that cues then had no tips and rails were made of cloth instead of rubber. White refers to another shark he once saw in Hamburg, in what is now West Germany, who could make balls jump from one table to another.

Betting on trick shots is a form of pool hustling, and the records of that go back even further. A hundred years before balls were zig-zagging across tables in Paris and flying through the air in Hamburg, a hustler was working his way through the French royal court, emptying silk purses by losing the first game and then raising the stakes, a strategy that still works today. According to billiard historian William Hendricks, who cites the 1695 memoirs of the Duke of St Simon, this particular hustler went on to achieve a distinction rare for a member of his profession. He became a Catholic bishop. No one knows if he continued to hustle pool while dressed as a prince of the church, but it would have been a great scam.

Hustling pool and everything else about the game was revolutionized in the early 1800s by a prison inmate who was once a captain in the French infantry. While languishing behind bars in an institution that felicitously featured a billiard table, Monsieur Mingaud, who did not give us his first name, discovered that the addition of a leather tip to his cue enabled him to spin the cueball, which profoundly affected its and

According to unverified information in Ripley's files, the money was lost in a single afternoon to the sovereign's chamberlain, one Barthels, which must make today's hustlers feel that they were born 280 years too late. The loss bankrupted Max.

his behavior. Legend has it that he stayed beyond the end of his sentence to finish his explorations of an undreamed-of wonderland and perfect his technique. When sprung at last he became the world's first professional exhibition player. He created a sensation in the courts, billiard salons, and public rooms of England and the Continent with his wizardry. Nobody had ever seen a cueball curve before or bounce off rails at such spooky angles.

Mingaud's 1827 book contains forty-five of his greatest shots and establishes him as one of the greatest innovators of all time in any field. It is truly remarkable how quickly and deeply he saw into the possibilities of his discovery. The 1830 English edition of his work is now very rare. There are only two copies in the United States that I know of, one at the Library of Congress and one at the University of Notre Dame.

While Captain Mingaud was the first and perhaps the best professional shooter of trick shots, he certainly wasn't the last. Examples of the breed can be found wherever the game is played. People love to watch as well as try trick shots. They love to see every ball on the table go into pockets like a dream come true, and they love to see a cueball behave as if it had a mind of its own. Because of public interest, it is possible to make a living as an exhibition player, provided you have enough skill and the right kind of personality. There is money to be made giving trick-shot shows at schools, clubs, tournaments, and even shopping centers. Pool shows on television almost always include a few fancy shots.

Sixty years ago Ralph Greenleaf was making $2,000 a week on the Orpheum circuit demonstrating his artistry with the aid of an overhead mirror that gave the audience a full view of the table. At the same time, the deep boondocks were being worked by at least a dozen "masked marvels," who in exchange for a fee would beat the local champ and show a few trick shots. There were specialists in shooting behind the back, one-handed, and in the case of George H. Sutton, *no*-handed (he had lost his hands and wrists in an accident as a youth, but could still run a thousand points in straight billiards). One Henry Lewis, Robert Ripley tells us, made a run of forty-six in straight billiards shooting only with his nose.

Today there are a dozen or so players who make all or most of their income as exhibition players, and in my opinion there is room for many more. There are school, tavern, commercial, and institutional markets that are almost untouched in many parts of the country. Readers interested in supplementing their incomes must be warned, however, that success as an exhibition player requires more than skill with a cue and a repertoire of shots. You have to be *entertaining*. Giving a trick-shot demonstration is a form of show business. This book will give you the repertoire; the showmanship is up to you.

When practicing the diagrammed shots, remember that balls, cloth, and cushions vary widely. I tested each shot before putting pen to paper, but the several tables I used might differ considerably from yours. Try it the recommended way first, then vary the hit, the English, the speed, and the ball placements to suit your conditions. This takes time and concentration on the more difficult shots, and only the hardest-working students will succeed.

In arranging a cluster, sometimes the balls won't stay put. Take another ball and hammer them into place. That not only teaches them their assigned positions, it makes it easy to set the shot up again because the balls will settle into the preformed pits. Make use of diamonds, pieces of chalk, and other aiming aids during practice. Unless you notice where the butt crosses the rail or at what point the cue is directed, you won't be able to repeat the shot exactly, and time will be wasted. Just fooling around is fun, but if you are trying to master a tough shot it pays to be as systematic as possible.

Do you need help with such fundamentals as grip, bridge, stance, aiming, and stroke? You won't find it here. There are several fine books on the market that deal with basics. The most comprehensive is *Byrne's Standard Book of Pool and Billiards*. The most inexpensive is *Winning Pocket Billiards,* by Willie Mosconi. The newest is *Winning Pool and Trick Shots,* by Nick Varner.

If you don't have time right now to get to a bookstore or a billiard-supply retailer, here are a few emergency suggestions. If the shot calls for hitting the cueball off center, your tip must be shaped and chalked properly. The curvature of a quarter is about right. To apply spin with security, you must learn to make a snug bridge with your forefinger looped over the cue. When you hit the cueball, follow straight through, don't let your cue rise in the air after impact.

Finally, if you know an unusual shot that isn't included here, especially one you invented yourself, send me a sketch in care of the publisher. In future editions there may be room for you.

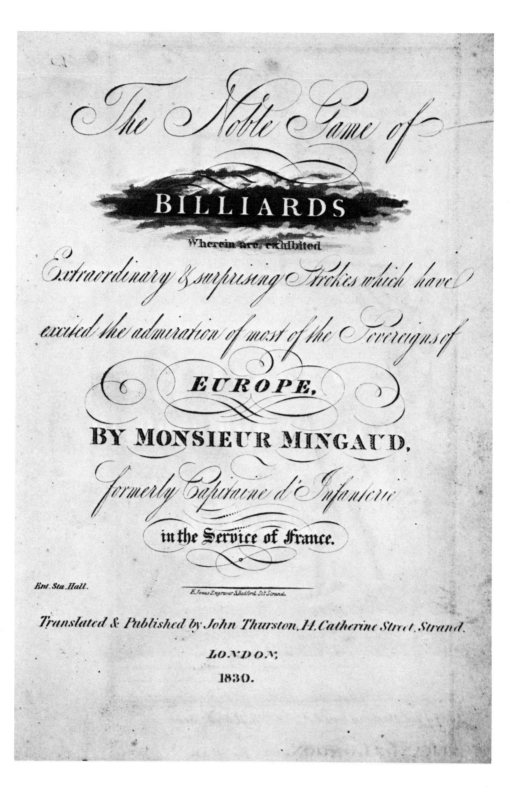

The Noble Game of

BILLIARDS

Wherein are exhibited

Extraordinary & surprising Strokes which have

excited the admiration of most of the Sovereigns of

EUROPE,

BY MONSIEUR MINGAUD,

formerly Capitaine d'Infanterie

in the Service of France.

Ent. Sta. Hall.

E. Jones Engraver 8 Bedford Sv. Strand.

Translated & Published by John Thurston, 14, Catherine Street, Strand.

LONDON;

1830.

Title page of history's first book of trick shots

POOL

1

Ten Classic Shots

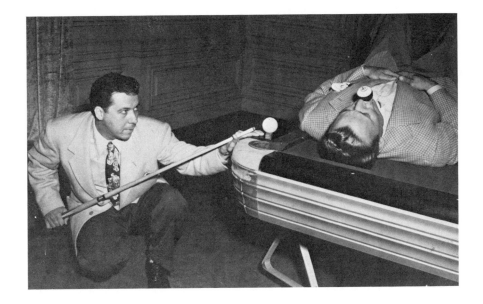

Jimmy Caras in *Super Cue Men*
(MGM, 1946)

Once invented, some trick shots are best forgotten; others endure and become a permanent part of a people's culture. Truly great shots, like the ten described in this chapter, demonstrate principles of physics in surprising ways, don't take forever to set up, can be made more than half the time by a good player, and have an exhilarating effect on spectators. Purified and refined in countless exhibitions, they are hard to improve. The only criticism one can make of them is that they have become, like Beethoven's Fifth Symphony and Prokofiev's March from *The Love of Three Oranges,* a little too familiar. For audiences that have never seen or heard them, though, they are dynamite.

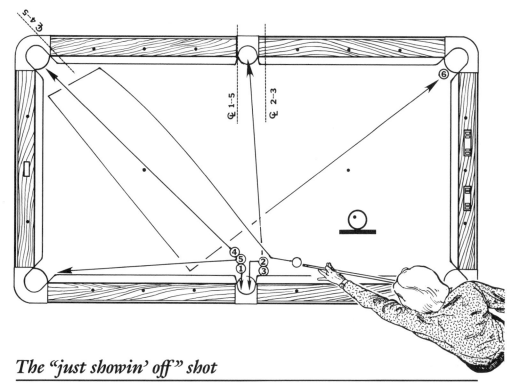

The "just showin' off" shot

This shot has been seen by more people by far than any other because it was the climax of an oft-repeated Miller Lite television commercial. It's not true that it took Steve Mizerak 181 tries to make it—that number of takes was required for the whole commercial, which featured a sequence of three trick shots integrated with dialogue, all filmed without cutting away. (The sequence is given on page 213, a variation with twelve balls on page 214.) Mizerak, who once won four straight U.S. Open straight pool titles, can make all six balls at least three-fourths of the time.

In the diagram, the dashed lines indicate how to orient the two-ball combinations. The enlarged cueball in the lower right part of the table shows the correct English. In arranging the balls, make sure that the one-five pair is slightly closer to the middle of table than the two-three so that the two will kiss off the five into the side pocket.

The shot was invented at least thirty years ago, nobody knows by whom.

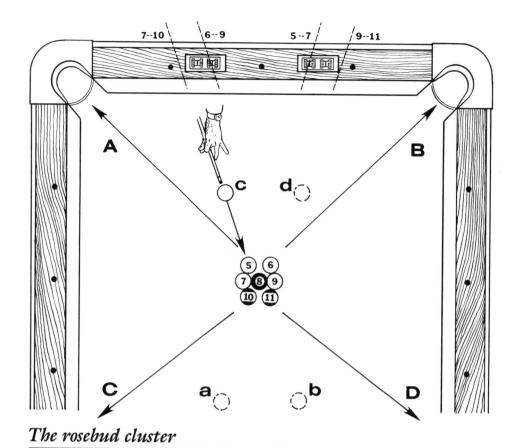

The rosebud cluster

Even though the eight-ball is surrounded, it can be made in any one of four pockets. If a spectator asks for side pocket C, place the cueball at c, as diagrammed. Striking the five-ball full clears the seven and ten out of the way and makes the eight kiss off the eleven. To make the eight in A, start from a, and so on. Once you know the required gap between the five and six and between the ten and eleven, the cluster can be set up in a flash. The shot is so automatic that it can be made by a volunteer from the bleachers. Cover the cluster with a handkerchief to heighten the mystery.

It's a shame that the creator of this lovely concept is lost to history. It goes back at least to the early 1930s, when Jimmy Caras saw Andrew Ponzi perform it. Some feel it should be credited to Onofrio Lauri.

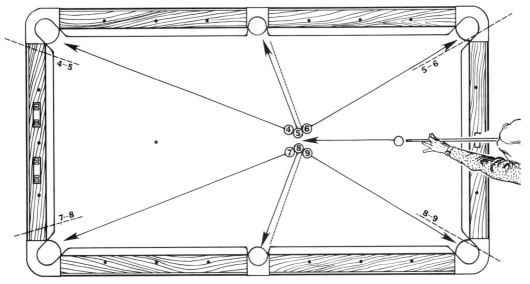

The butterfly formation

Hit the diagrammed arrangement as indicated and you'll make a ball in each of the six pockets, which can't be said about any other trick shot. The space between the five and eight should be about two-thirds the width of a ball. Note that the six and nine are a hair beyond the first diamond from the side pocket.

The shot goes back at least to 1918, when *Trick and Fancy Pocket Billiard Shots,* by Anonymous, was published (see Bibliography), a book I will refer to henceforth simply as Anonymous.

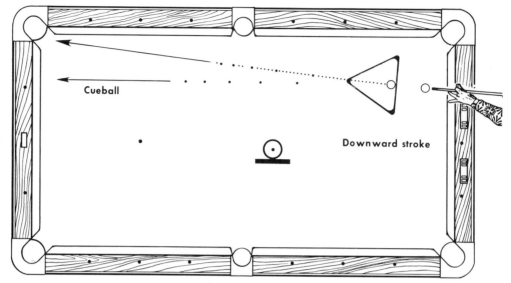

Cueball

Downward stroke

The jump-out-of-the-rack shot

That a cueball leaves the table when struck a downward blow has been known for at least two hundred years; demonstrating the fact with the aid of a triangle goes back to before the turn of the century. Despite the stunt's antiquity, there is always a freshman class that has never seen it. It does seem impossible that an object ball can be jumped out of the triangle and pocketed in the corner without touching the triangle, yet average players with practice can learn to make it. The cue must be elevated to an angle of about forty-five degrees and the cueball hit with considerable force. The distance between the cueball and the object ball should be about a foot, though that varies with the force, the cue angle, and the flexibility of the table bed. A flimsy bed acts like a trampoline.

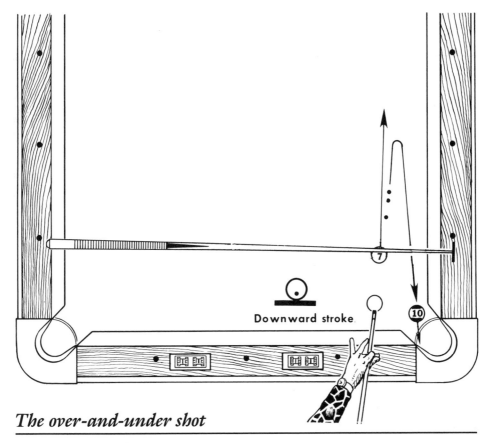

Downward stroke.

The over-and-under shot

With the proper buildup, this can be a feature of any trick-shot show. The idea has been around at least since 1890, when Professor J.F.B. McCleery of the San Francisco Olympic Club published his manual on the game. The seven-ball is made in the corner pocket, the cueball jumps over the rake, goes a foot or so forward, then returns under the rake to pocket the ten. You have to elevate the cue about thirty degrees and hit the cueball below center.

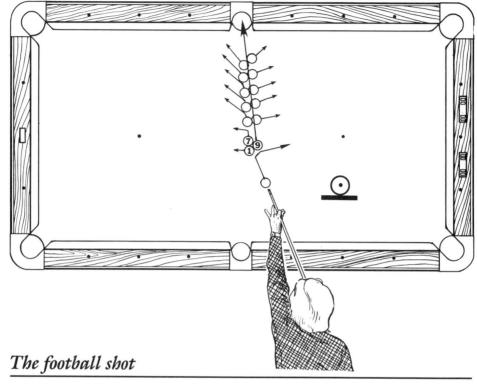

The football shot

Downfield blocking clears the way for the halfback carrying the ball, hence the football shot. Whoever thought of the idea of pairing balls this way so they would divide on impact deserves a government pension, because it is one of the great trick-shot themes. It might have been Charlie Peterson, a tireless exhibition player and billiard missionary who was active from 1910 to the late 1950s. In the diagram, the cueball makes the nine in the side by caroming into it off the one. The seven hits the first pair of interference balls, setting up a chain reaction that splits them all. For a scholarly audience you might consider a reference to Exodus 14:21. Be sure to cut the one away from the nine so that the nine stays put for the carom.

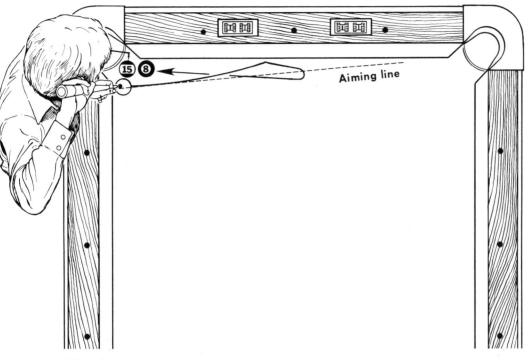

Aiming line

The short massé

Among massé shots, this is one of the easiest, yet it can provoke tremendous audience response. The diagram shows the idea in its easiest form. The fifteen is in the jaws and can be pocketed by the cueball without touching the eight. The way the cueball spurts along the rail a foot or two before stopping and reversing direction to sink the eight provides wholesome entertainment for the entire family, including Sis and Gramps. The farther the cueball goes before reversing the better, the distance being a function of the speed of stroke, the slipperiness of the cloth and cueball, and the angle of elevation. To minimize cueball travel and the chance of error, hold the cue almost vertical. (From Anonymous, 1918.)

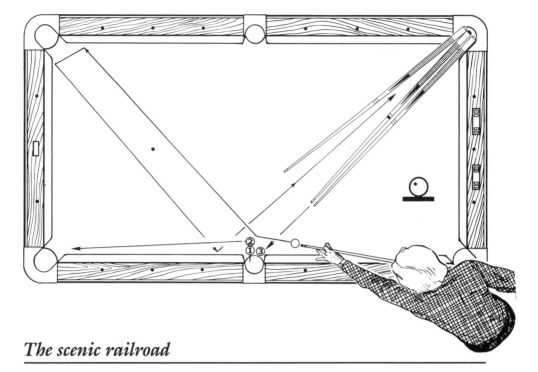

The scenic railroad

Guaranteed to make even the most torpid audience laugh, clap, and squeal is the scenic railroad shot, also called the cable car shot and, by Mike Massey, the Chattanooga choo-choo. The skill required is minimal. All you need is some ability at judging cueball speed. After knocking the two in the corner and the one in the side, the cueball, aided by running English (in this case, left), banks off three rails, rides up between two of the three cues, turns the corner at the pocket, runs downhill between the other two cues and pockets the three. Shoot too softly and the cueball won't climb the grade; too hard and the cueball runs up the cues and leaps to its death on the floor.

The shot is thought to be quite old. Herrmann doesn't mention it in his 1902 book, although his switchback carom lacks only the charming turn-the-corner feature. Jimmy Caras recalls learning the shot in 1926 from an old man at the Wilmington, Delaware, YMCA. In setting up the shot, make sure the tips of the lower two cues are lined up evenly, otherwise the emerging cueball will be thrown off course.

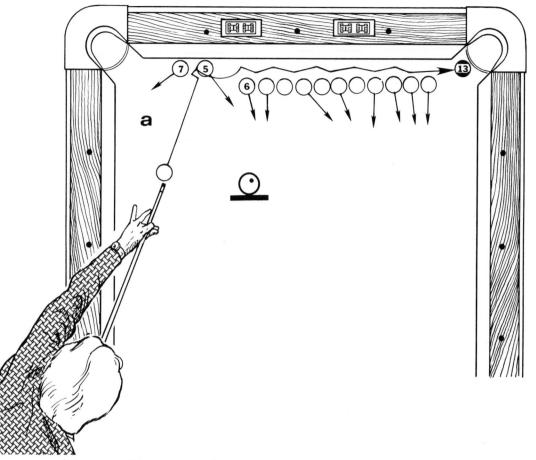

The machine-gun shot

In *Winning Pocket Billiards* (1965), Willie Mosconi called this shot the machine gun because of the chattering sound made when the cueball fights its way toward the thirteen behind the line of balls. A good stroke is needed. Hit the five full with maximum high right English, slightly on the left side. After bouncing off the five into the seven, the cueball embarks on a deeply satisfying struggle along the rail.

Billiard players might wish to try the shot with the cueball at a, in which case the seven can be dispensed with. The row of balls should be a little more than a ball space from the rail.

The shoot-off-your-mouth shot

Take four pieces of chalk. Put one, exposed side up, between the teeth of a volunteer, whom you arrange as shown. Stack the other three in the middle of the rail. Put the eight-ball on the single piece and the cueball on the stack. Drop to one knee and shoot up at the eight-ball, pocketing it in the corner. Shoot softly enough to allow the cueball to dribble harmlessly down the cheek to the table. This is a sensational shot and a perfect closer for an exhibition program. Done properly, the volunteer will not be seriously injured and will be able to return under his own power to his loved ones, if any.

Red Jones of Saint Petersburg, Florida, thought of the shot in 1970 after trick golfer Joe Kirkwood drove a golf ball off his mouth. Staten Island's Pete Margo invented the shot independently in 1976 when it occurred to him that a human head could be substituted for the bottle he usually used. When he performed it on ABC's "Wide World of Sports" in 1978, the human head belonged to Al Rosen, who had already broken his nose seventeen times stopping baseballs at third base for the Cleveland Indians.

But Jimmy Caras has both Jones and Margo beat. Caras can be seen doing the shot in the 1946 movie short *Super Cue Men*. (See page 3.)

2

Ten Classic Variations

Aquatic billiards at Atlantic City's Ambassador Hotel.

In the relentless march of Western civilization and Japan, everything tends to get meddled with. Well enough is seldom left alone. The result is not always an improvement, but at least it is new, which sells. In the last chapter, pool balls were used to express certain ideas. The ideas can be expressed in other ways with the same balls, as we will now see.

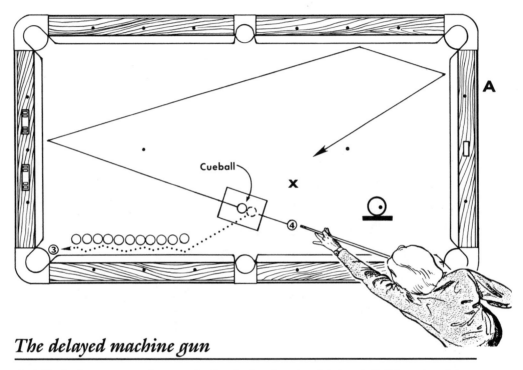

The delayed machine gun

A skilled player can make a cueball spin in place by driving it full into an object ball with English (not follow or draw). If you can do it, this shot is for you. In the diagram, the rectangle represents a sheet of paper, mylar, plastic, or glass, which cuts down on the friction between the spinning ball and the cloth. Place the cueball on the rectangle and drive the four-ball into it with maximum right English. A good hit will leave the four spinning in place. Quickly reposition yourself at A, grab the cueball as it comes off the third rail and place it at X. Now hit the cueball into the four so that the four follows the dotted line to pocket the three. Without the friction reducer the four will be too sluggish to do its job. (Byrne.)

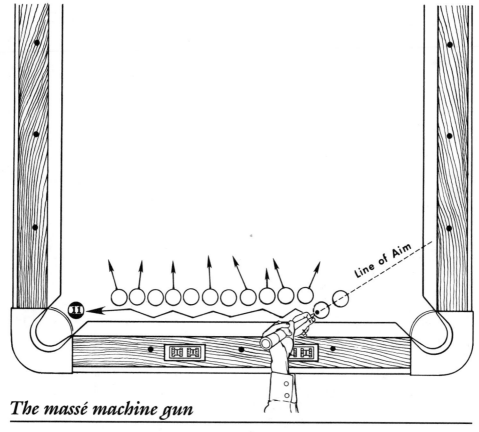

The massé machine gun

If you have a good massé stroke, you might be able to make the machine-gun shot with massé alone. The idea goes back fifty years.

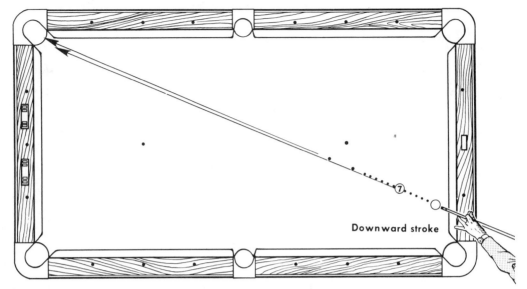

Downward stroke

The accelerated jump shot

Jumping a ball out of the triangle is nice (see page 8), but old. Diagrammed is Captain Mingaud's version, which appears in his 1827 book. Build your bridge on the rail so that you can easily stroke downward at the cueball. The cueball and the seven-ball must be precisely lined up with the corner pocket. Jump over the seven, grazing it with cueball so that both balls go into the corner pocket, *cueball first*.

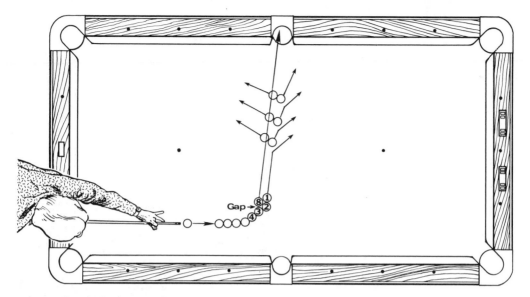

The left-turn football shot

In this early version of the football shot, the eight-ball goes into the side pocket. The three pairs of would-be tacklers are taken out by the one-ball. Charlie Peterson can be seen doing it this way in *Popular Mechanics* magazine in 1934 (month unknown, but the page number is 696), which was sent to me by Jess Meshanic of Metuchen, New Jersey. Note closely the arrangement of the numbered balls. Set up like this, the one-ball pops out first followed by the eight-ball. The gap between the eight and three helps. Crucial is the slight curve formed by the two, three, and eight. Contemporary trick-shot inventors should be able to exploit this forgotten concept.

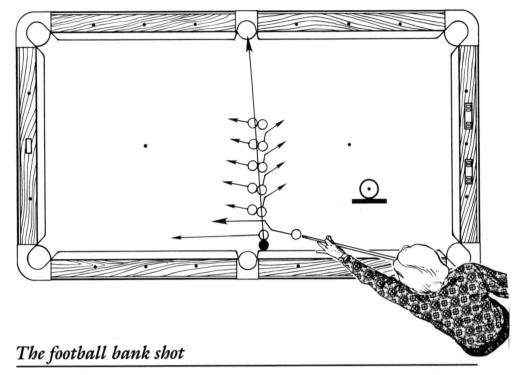

The football bank shot

Definitely a better version than the classic set-up given in Chapter One. Unfortunately, it's slightly more difficult. The black ball here is the one that goes, banking across into the side pocket. Fred Whelan of Hollywood, California, the former Pacific Coast pool champion, who is now in his eighties, leads into the shot with a story about how O. J. Simpson seems hopelessly trapped behind the line.

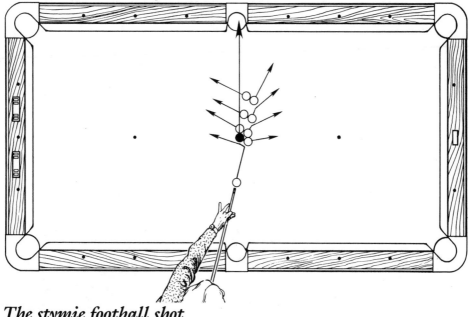

The stymie football shot

Paul Gerni showed me this version. Again it is the black ball that goes, propelled by the cueball caroming off the first ball. Be sure to cut the first ball away from the black. The four-ball cluster makes a good shot by itself; the uninformed can't see how the black ball can be made. (See page 76.)

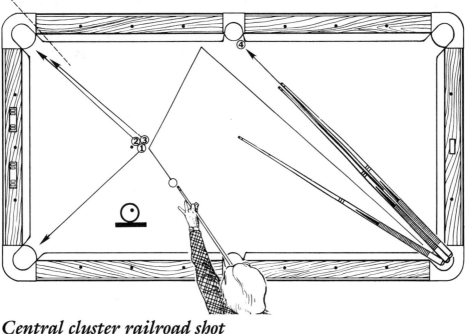

Central cluster railroad shot

If you can make all three balls in a cluster arranged as shown in the left of the diagram, then you are ready for this version of a beloved classic. It's well suited to undersized tavern tables.

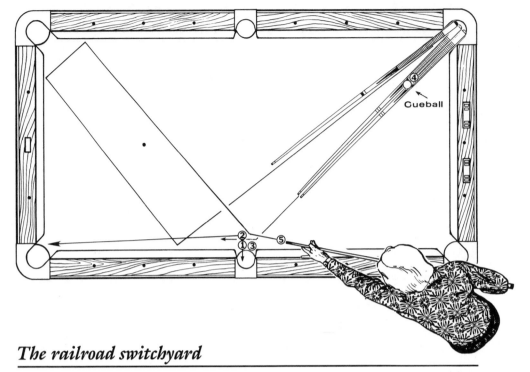

The railroad switchyard

I love this. Five balls are made in sequence in an unpredictable and delightful manner. In the diagram, the cueball and the four-ball are held in place on the cues by a match or a small piece of folded paper. Shoot with the five-ball, as shown. The one drops first, then the two. The five travels three rails, climbs the grade into the roundhouse, turns the corner, and collides with the four. The impact dislodges the paper match, and the three balls begin to roll downhill, slowly gathering speed. The cueball, several inches ahead of the four when they leave the cues, knocks in the three and gets out of the way to let the four and five follow the three into the side. What more can you ask of a trick shot? I wish I could name the inventor.

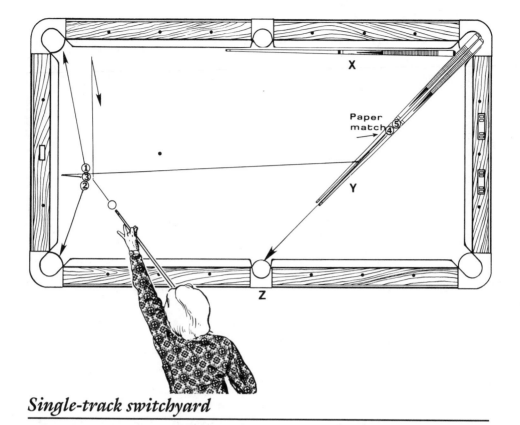

Single-track switchyard

Fred Whelan showed me this method of making five balls in sequence. Practice first just with three balls until you can make the one and two and send the three straight up the table. In the diagram, the four and five are precariously held in place by a paper match. The cue at X helps steady the other two cues, an idea of Paul Lucchesi, Sr.'s. After you pull the trigger, quickly place your right hand on the cues at Y to steady them. The speed must be such that the three-ball will climb on top of the cues and run uphill to nudge the four without jumping over both cues. Once the paper match is dislodged, the three balls run down the single track into the side pocket. Thanks, Fred. (See also the novelty variation on page 98.)

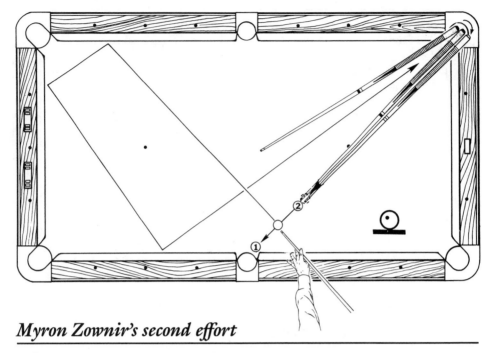

Myron Zownir's second effort

Who says there's nothing new? Get a load of the nifty nuance Myron Zownir has added to a standard classic. By precise placement of the two-ball, Zownir, a veteran trick-shot explorer from Long Island City, New York, has created a pleasing second-effort effect. The cueball bounces off three rails, climbs the cues, turns the corner as usual, and rolls downhill to hit the two, which moves forward to knock the one into the pocket. The two stops and waits after hitting the one; the cueball, on the other hand, still has a little life in it because when it hit the two *it was still on the cues*. Falling off the cuetips gives the cueball enough momentum to trickle forward and pocket the two. Clever. I'm impressed, Myron.

3
Wisdom of the Ancients

Michael Phelan, from his book *The Game of Billiards* (1858). It was Phelan who wrote: "Look, ladies, at the billiard table as a means of domesticating your husbands . ˙. . as a means of making home so agreeable that they will seldom leave it except on business or in your society."

The wisdom of the ancients can be found in such books as *Noble Jeu de Billard* (Paris, 1827) by Captain Mingaud, The Game of Billiards (New York, 1858) by Michael Phelan, *The McCleery Method of Billiard Playing* (San Francisco, 1890) by Professor J.F.B. McCleery, and *Fun on the Pool Table* (New York, 1902) by Fred Herrmann. The first three are extremely rare; the last is readily available in paperback from Dover Publications under the title *Tricks and Games on the Pool Table* (New York, 1967). Read all four and you'll see that much of what we know today about what can be done with pool and billiard balls was known by the turn of the century. In short, those old geezers could *play*.

Phelan doesn't devote much space to trick shots, and many of Herrmann's seventy-eight items are closer to jokes and juggling than what we think of today as trick shots. Some of the feats described in Mingaud and McCleery, though, strain one's faculties of belief. They would severely tax the skill of the greatest players of any era. Some of Mingaud's shots were so amazing, especially in the days when hardly anybody had ever seen a spinning cueball (he was the first to put a leather tip on his cue), that the publisher of the English edition of his book, John Thurston, saw fit to swear that he had seen the fabulous Frenchman make every one.

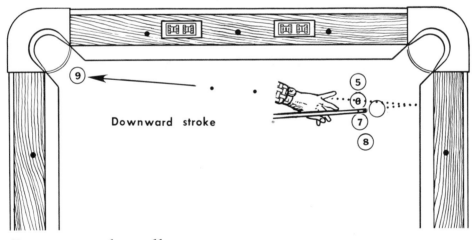

Escape over the wall

Many of today's exhibition players use this shot in their acts. How many of them realize how elderly it is? Mingaud diagrammed it for his book in 1827. The cueball is trapped behind a row of balls, and the object is to pocket the nine-ball without touching the interference. Elevate the cue between twenty and thirty degrees, and strike the cueball a downward blow, which will make it leap over the wall after rebounding from the rail. The necessary courage and assertiveness comes with practice. For shots requiring this much elevation of the cue, use an open rather than a looped (forefinger on top) bridge.

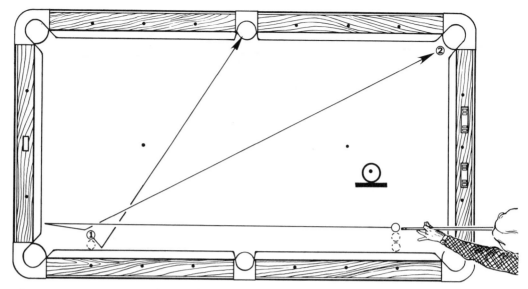

Captain Mingaud's bank carom

Place the balls as shown. (The dashed circles represent ball spaces.) Announce that the one-ball will go in the upper side pocket and the two-ball in the upper right corner. See if anybody can figure out how that could be done. A hundred and fifty years ago, Captain Mingaud was doing it by going to the end rail first. It's not a high-percentage shot, but it's not quite as unlikely as it looks. Think how tough it was for Mingaud, who was faced with bigger tables, smaller pockets, and lousy cushions. (Vulcanized rubber was decades away.)

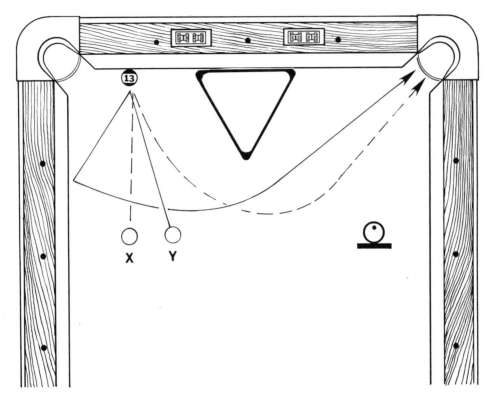

Two tough kiss-back follow shots

I'm glad I wasn't hanging around the salons of Paris 160 years ago, because I would have lost all my money betting that Captain Mingaud couldn't make these two extremely difficult shots. The thirteen is frozen on the rail. From position X, the cueball is directed at the thirteen, slightly right of center, with extreme follow and a hard stroke. What you hope will happen is that the cueball will follow the dashed line around the triangle (Mingaud used a high silk hat) into the upper right pocket. From position Y, hit the thirteen slightly left of center and try to make the cueball hit the side rail before curving into the right-hand pocket. Mingaud used to make these shots with the cueball at the other end of the table. Some player!

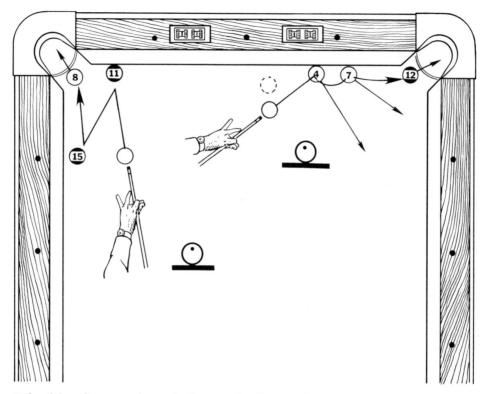

The kiss-forward and the push-through

At the left is a great idea from Mingaud that lamentably has been forgotten and that I am proud to reintroduce. Kiss back from the frozen eleven-ball with high follow; if you can manage to hit the fifteen-ball fairly full, the cueball will spurt forward toward the eight-ball. The shot is not too tough at short range like this. Mingaud diagrams it with the fifteen another diamond away. At the right is a severe test from Professor McCleery. Hit the four-ball full with follow, English slightly left. The idea is for the cueball to bank the four out of the way, then to dive onto the seven, knocking it out of the way as well, finally moving along the rail to pocket the twelve. Very tough. With the cueball in the position of the dashed circle, it's easier and not so pretty. From that angle the four takes the seven out, clearing the way for the cueball to follow straight through to the twelve.

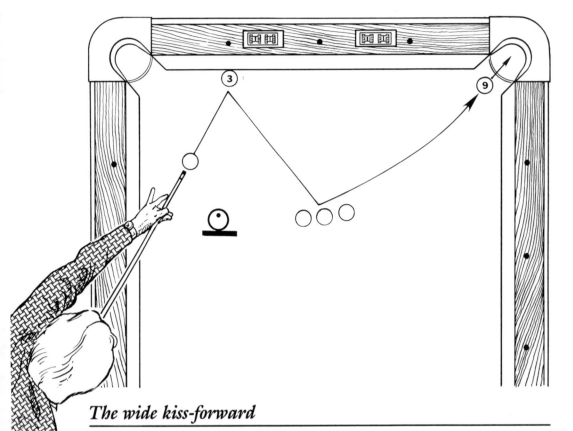

The wide kiss-forward

Michael Phelan's *Billiards Without a Master* (1850) and *The Game of Billiards* (1858) were the first American books on the game. I've never seen the former, but as I write, my elbow is on the latter, holding it open to page 126, where a diagram similar to the one above appears. At Mike Massey's suggestion, I have added a couple of extra "bankboard" balls to increase the margin of error. As you can see, it's an application of Mingaud's kiss-forward idea from the previous diagram.

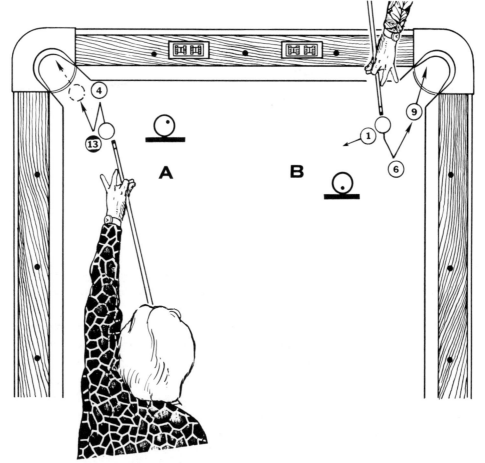

The relocation kiss-forward and the triangular draw

At the left is my version of the kiss-forward theme. If right English is applied to the cueball as well as follow, the frozen ball is squeezed to the left to be met by the returning cueball. The better you are, the farther away the thirteen can be. Start your practice with the thirteen as shown, or even closer to the four. At the right is what I have named the triangular draw. If you can draw from the six to the nine, then you ought to be able to feather the one on the way to the six. The diagram shows a possible application in a game of nine-ball. In Phelan's 1858 diagram, the four balls form a square, a much harder starting position. (Also see page 190.)

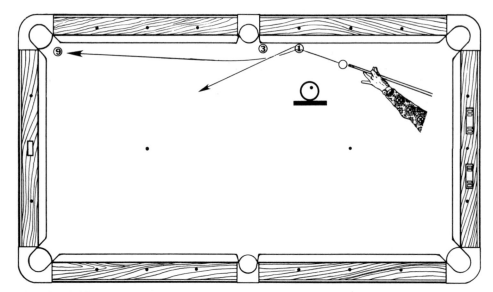

Force follow around a ball

The nineteenth-century masters were well aware of what happens when a cueball with various spins and speeds strikes a ball frozen to a rail. Phelan diagrams several shots in which the cueball bends around an interfering ball. Here is one of the easiest, which doesn't mean it is easy. To get the required action, make sure you hit the one-ball squarely in the face. Your tip should be well chalked and you must strike the cueball far above center.

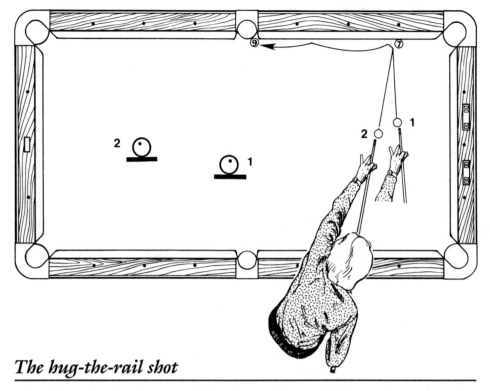

The hug-the-rail shot

The object is to hit the seven full and make the cueball move along the rail to pocket the nine. From position one, you need only follow on the cueball and no sidespin. From position two, left English is needed as well as follow. (Phelan.)

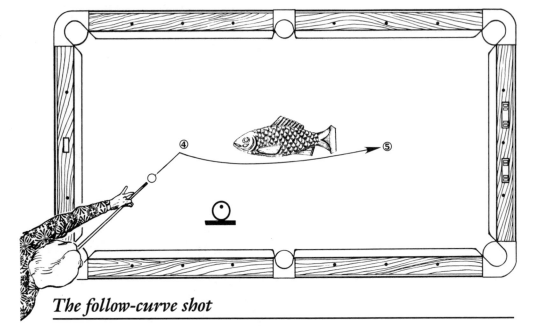

The follow-curve shot

Place the four-ball on the head spot, the five-ball on foot spot, and a frozen flounder in the center of the table. If you strike the four about half full with follow, the cueball will curve around the flounder to hit the five, a useful demonstration to beginners of the effect of follow on cut shots. Anything can be used as an obstacle. I used a flounder because I happened to have one handy. Michael Phelan, playing in the days before refrigeration, used a hat.

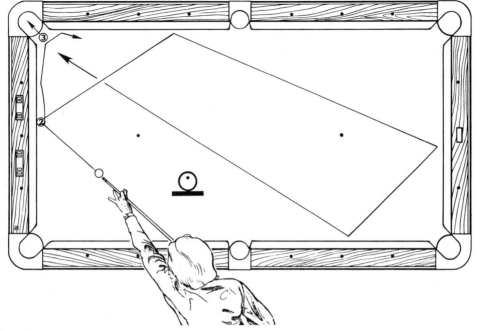

Michael Phelan's challenge

With the balls in this position, can the two and three be made in the upper left corner? Michael Phelan once asked that of the readers of a paper called *Billiard Cue*. "It seems simple now," he writes in *The Game of Billiards*, "when the lines are drawn, but when the proposition first appeared . . . many attempts were made before the stroke was finally accomplished by one of our most distinguished amateurs." The shot is widely known now and was used a couple of years ago as part of skill-shot competition among top American players. Phelan got no credit for having invented it, possibly because nobody involved in the event ever heard of him.

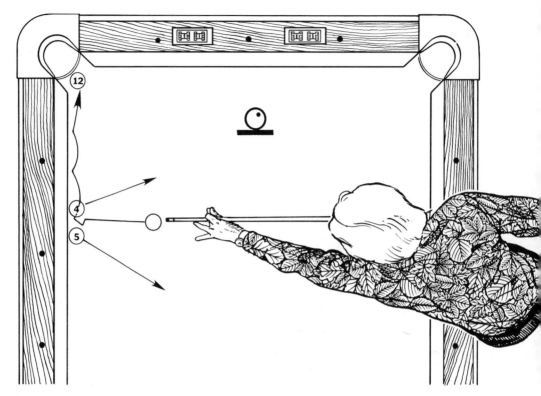

Professor McCleery's creep

Place two balls about an inch and a half apart, frozen to a rail or close to it. The cueball is perpendicular to the gap a foot or two away. Shoot hard with high right English, trying for a simultaneous hit, and watch the cueball hug the rail and pocket a ball in the corner. It doesn't seem to make much difference which ball you hit first, but I like favoring the four-ball, as drawn above. Professor McCleery calls this the creep shot in his 1890 book. He did it with the balls on the end rail and the cueball at the opposite end of the table.

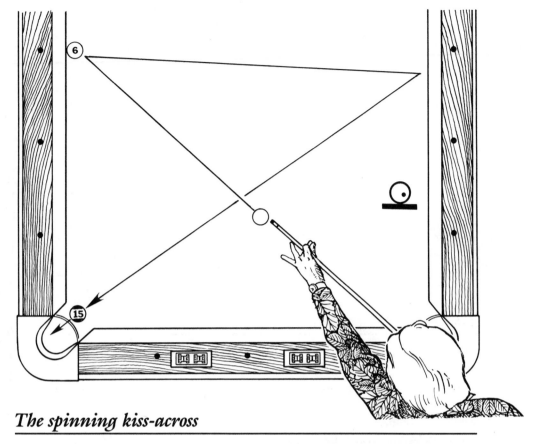

The spinning kiss-across

Use low right and hit the frozen six-ball a hair to the right of dead center. The object is to make the cueball kiss back off the six and travel almost straight across the table to the opposite rail, where the right spin takes effect. With luck, you'll make the fifteen. McCleery presents this as a position shot in straight billiards; the six tends to bank three rails and join the other two.

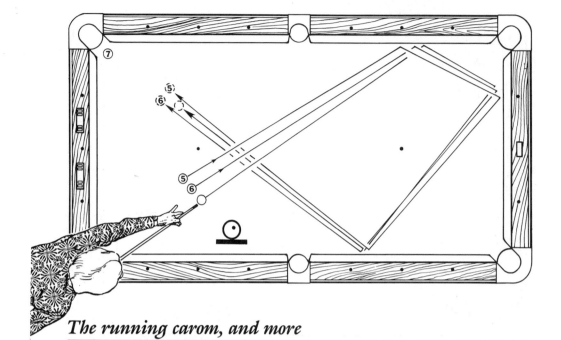

The running carom, and more

This is my adaptation to pool of a billiard shot Professor McCleery called the running carom. In his version, two object balls and the cueball are banked three rails one after the other; the cueball catches up to the others and makes a carom. Tell the audience you will not only do that but pocket the seven-ball as well. The diagram shows an ideal scenario: the cueball splits the side-by-side object balls and continues forward to make the seven. There are dozens of ways the conditions can be met, which makes the shot easier than it looks. Whenever you get a successful result, pretend that's the way you played it. In the diagram, shoot the five first, then the six, then the cueball, all with running English. With practice you will learn how to vary the speeds to bring about a reunion in the upper left corner.

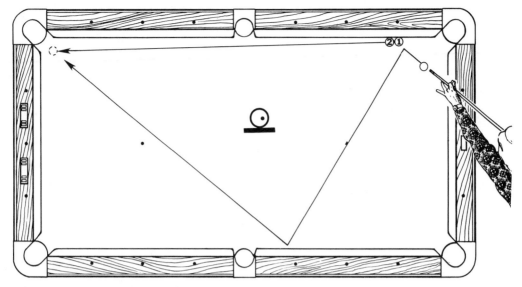

The kiss-across time shot

Eight editions of *Modern Billiards,* by H. W. Collender, were published in New York between 1881 and 1912. The 103 diagrams in the first edition (in later editions the number of diagrams is reduced to make room for more match results) are entirely devoted to the most popular game of the day, three-ball straight billiards on a pocketless table. Many of the "gather" shots, in which a carom is made and the three balls are brought together, often by the most ingenious means, could be adapted to pool. An example is given above. Kiss back off the one-ball and try to knock the two-ball into the corner while it's still moving. Very tough, although merely making the carom isn't so bad.

Twenty-five Easy Ones

It's quite a trick to make Mike Sigel, America's best tournament player, smile this broadly. A check for $30,000 and two slave girls will do it.

Trying to make the shots in the previous chapter is enough to break the spirit of all but the most obdurate. The shots in the two chapters before that aren't exactly cookies, either. Fortunately, there are a lot of entertaining shots that almost anyone can make, which is not to say that you don't have to know that the thick end of the cue is the rear. Twenty of them are diagrammed in this chapter to restore the confidence of the readers. Beginners should also check the books by Herrmann and Caras.

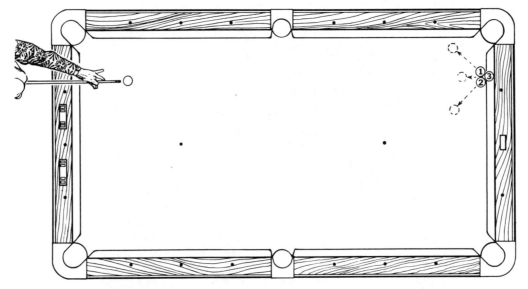

Fred Herrmann's slow collapse

Freeze the one and two against each other and the rail and balance the three on top of them as shown. With the cueball at the other end of the table announce that you will hit the three without touching the others. Don't make a bet, though, unless you have your victim under hypnosis, because the shot depends on cheating—cheating that is so obvious it is funny. Well, mildly amusing. Shoot the cueball very slowly toward the three, and while it's in motion kick or bump the table hard enough to dislodge the precarious equilibrium of the three-ball pyramid. The weight of the three pushes the one and two apart, and it rolls forward on the table to meet the inexorably advancing cueball. This is the first shot in Herrmann's book, and one of the best of his many nonshot or gag items. Unfortunately, 179,643,211 Americans have already seen it.

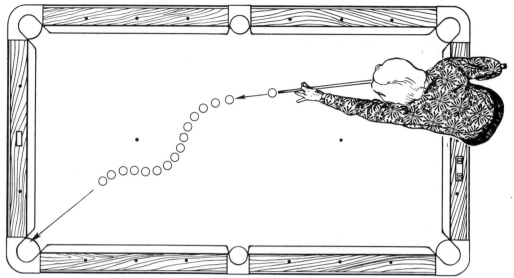

The fifteen-ball combination

Arrange the fifteen balls in a curve of your own devising, spacing them about a half ball apart, and making sure the last three form a dead combination. Shoot the cueball hard into the other end of the line and you've made a fifteen-ball combination, a peak you'll never attain in real life. It's worth shooting the shot just to hear the sound it makes, especially if you use thirty balls, as Wisconsin's Bruce Venzke does. The basic idea goes back to Anonymous, 1918.

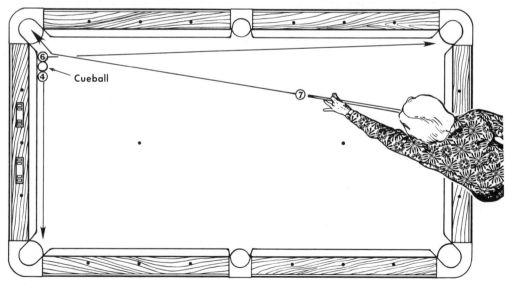

The paralyzed intermediary

In this shot the cueball is frozen between the four and six. Shoot the seven off the six into the corner pocket. The cueball helps guide the six so that it banks into the upper right pocket and it transmits force to the four, which goes into the lower left pocket, but it seems to do nothing. Correctly stroked, the cueball remains oddly rooted in place, moving not even a millimeter. If it drifts slightly, try moistening the contact points.

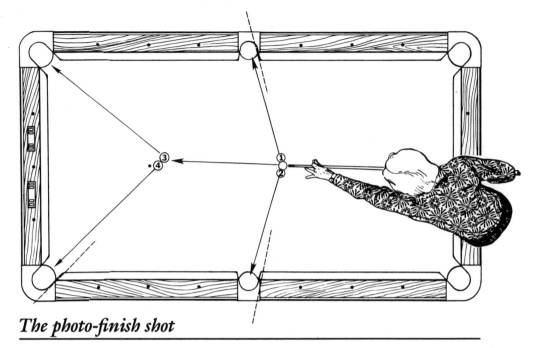

The photo-finish shot

The dashed lines show how to aim the two-ball combinations. Shoot straight ahead and the four balls go in almost simultaneously. Minnesota Fats usually lets a member of the audience shoot it. Covering the three-four with a handkerchief is a nice touch.

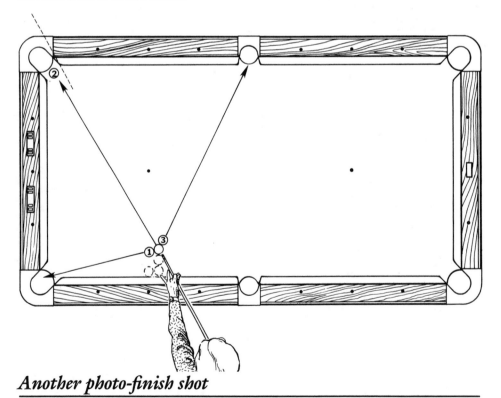

Another photo-finish shot

You would need a photo to see which ball finishes first. Dashed circles show where to set up the three-ball cluster. Aim along the dashed line.

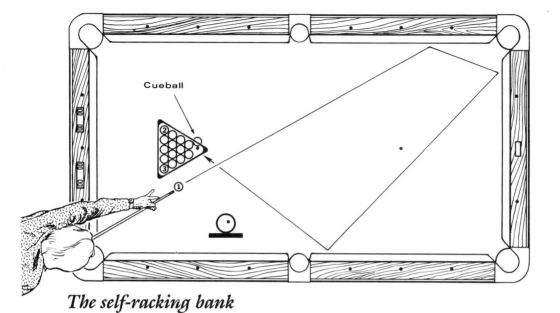

Cueball

The self-racking bank

In Willie Mosconi's *Winning Pocket Billiards,* this is called the lazy man's rack. The cueball is wedged under the triangle. The one-ball is banked, three cushions, and as it passes under the front of the triangle it knocks the cueball aside, allowing the triangle to drop to the table. When practicing, start with the one-ball in exactly the same position each time.

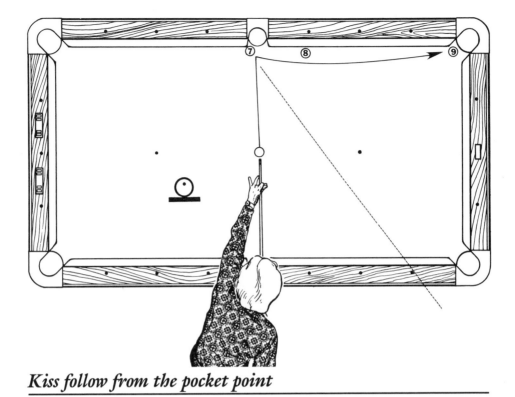

Kiss follow from the pocket point

This is one of the easiest ways to achieve a controlled cueball curve. Freeze the seven-ball against the point of the side pocket so that it is "aimed" along the dashed line. From the center of the table, aim for a half-ball hit on the seven. (In a half-ball hit, the line of aim projected forward touches the edge of the object ball.) Properly stroked, the cueball will curve around the eight and pocket the nine. The shot is diagrammed on a snooker table in *50 Best Trick Shots* (almost all of which are in Caras), by Ray Reardon of London, England, who suggests left English. Of course, being English himself, he calls it "side." Bill Marshall of Lynchburg, Virginia, suggests straight follow. Listen to Bill.

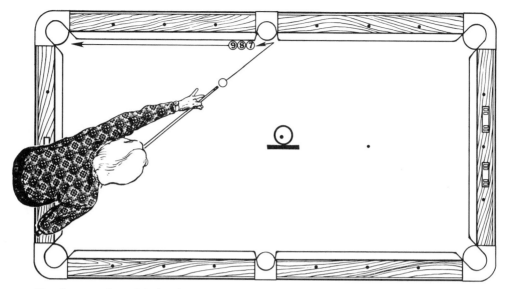

Pocket point kick shot

From this position, ask a friend to make the nine without banking the cueball to the right end rail. The simple solution is shown. It's slightly harder to omit the nine and make the eight, still harder to omit the nine and eight and make the seven. The idea can occasionally be used in games.

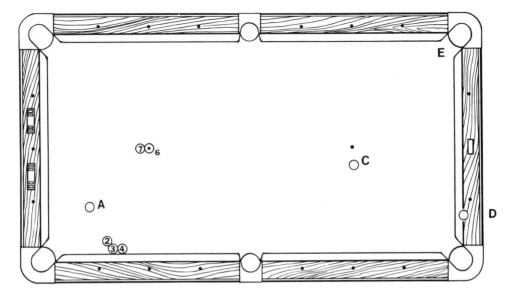

Three great spit shots

Not everybody has yet learned that moisture—as in spit—eliminates friction between frozen balls, and therefore the "throw" effect as well. The best demonstration is in the two-three-four cluster above. Hitting the two from cueball position A will cause the four to stay on the rail and drop in the lower right pocket, provided the contact point between the three and four has been moistened. Otherwise, the four leaves the rail and won't go in. People have been driven round the bend over this shot. Fortunes have changed hands. A lesser-known manifestation of the same principle, devised by Bill Marshall, calls for spotting the six and freezing the seven behind it. The cueball is at C. By hitting the six on the left, you can bank the seven to E or at least come within six inches of the pocket. The person you are betting against can't, because when you spot the balls for him you moisten the contact point, which keeps the seven on the centerline of the table. In other words, he'll miss by half the width of the table. Don't issue this challenge to those who can't handle impotence. A final example comes to us from Herrmann's 1902 opus. Put a cueball atop the rail at D. Lay a forefinger across it and press downward until the cueball squirts forward like a watermelon seed. If you secretly lick the pad of your finger, you can make the cueball hit the opposite end rail. Your hapless opponent will be lucky to get the cueball to go more than a foot because backspin will stop it in its tracks.

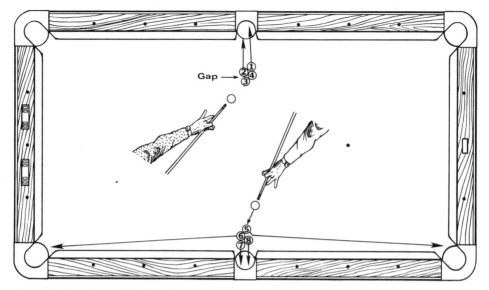

A subtle four-ball cluster

Study the one-two-three-four cluster at the top of the diagram. Hit the three full and both the one and two will go into the side pocket, but not unless you observe the details. Note that the cueball-three-four don't form a straight line and that there is a gap between the two and three. The idea is from an article on Charlie Peterson that appeared in a 1934 *Popular Mechanics* sent to me by Jess Meshanic. Searching for ways to extract more from the concept, I came up with the shot at the bottom of the diagram. All four balls are supposed to go, although there is no law that says they have to. You'll have to experiment with the exact positioning and the size of the gap.

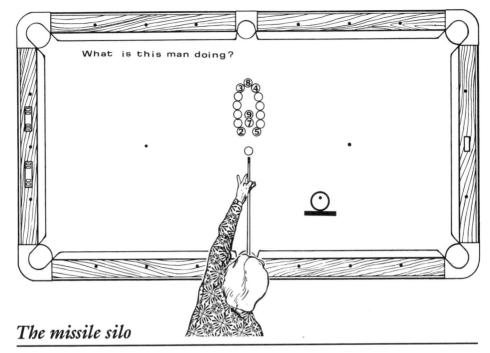

The missile silo

What the man is doing is shooting the missile silo shot, invented by the lovely and self-effacing author of this and many other splendid books. The nine-ball is the missile and the side pocket is the target. The missile's trajectory is blocked by the three, eight, and four. When the cueball is sent into the bottom of the silo, the three and four will diverge and the eight will go one way or another depending on which ball the cueball hits first. Delayed slightly by the two and five, the cueball triggers the seven-nine combination after the silo lid has been blown apart. The balls spread apart like the petals of a spring blossom. Maybe I should have called it the spring blossom shot. Adjust the gap between the two and five so that enough force is transmitted to the eight while still allowing the cueball to shoulder its way through.

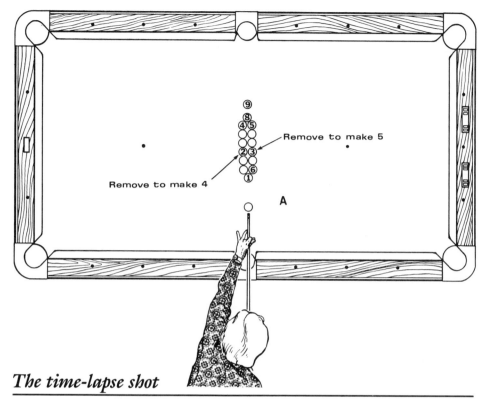

Remove to make 5

Remove to make 4

A

The time-lapse shot

I like this one, maybe because I thought of it. To make the five, remove the three-ball before shooting; to make the four, remove the two. If the two is gone, a ball must travel across the gap it leaves, which allows enough time for the other side of the pattern to clear away the five, eight, and nine. With the three gone, the four will take out the eight and nine before the forward impulse is transmitted to the five. The five can also be made without removing a ball by shooting the cueball from A. Hit the one almost full, caroming lightly into the six. The nine adds to the mystery, but must be located accurately. Leave it out if it causes you trouble.

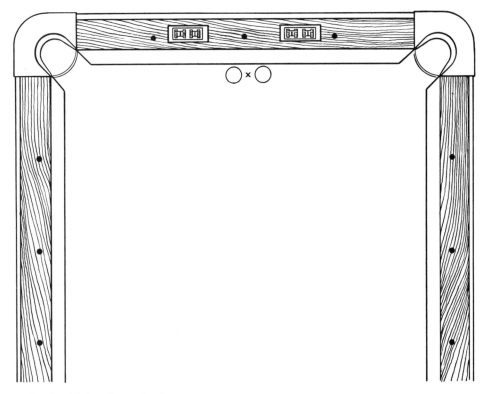

The ball-in-hand shot

Two balls about half a ball apart are at the middle of the end rail, not quite touching the rail. Hand a friend the cueball and say: "With ball in hand, make both balls." The trick is to hold the cueball about eight inches above point X and drop it. Stu Smith showed the shot to Bob Jewett, who showed it to me.

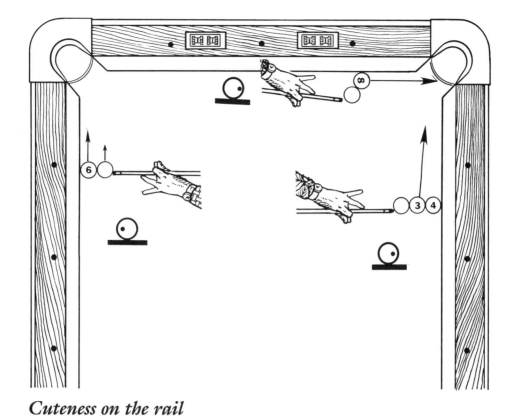

Cuteness on the rail

To make the six and three, place the cuetip against the cueball with the indicated English and slowly increase the pressure. Cogwheel action results and the balls squeeze into the pockets. The eight can be made by hitting the cueball so far to the right that you miscue.

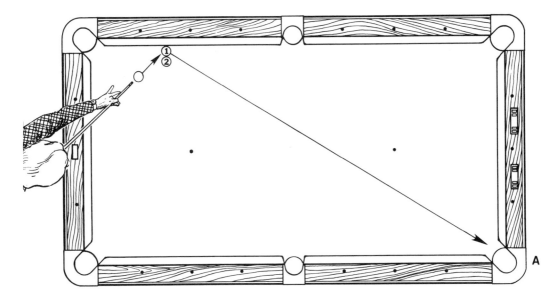

The optical-illusion bank

This is the first trick shot I ever learned. The one and two are frozen perpendicular to the rail. Announce that you will make the one in corner pocket A without touching or moving the two. It looks impossible to the uninitiated, even after they've seen it done. What happens is that the one sinks into the rail to get around the two. Shoot fairly hard and pretend the two isn't even there.

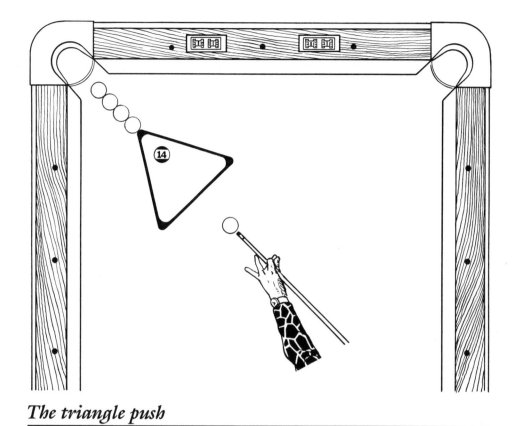

The triangle push

Without the triangle on the table, state that you will make the four frozen balls in the corner. Before shooting place the triangle as shown.

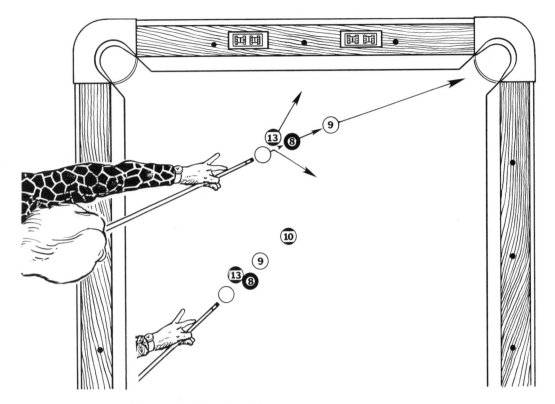

The hidden double-hit shot

If the cueball is within six or eight inches from an object ball that is straight into a pocket, you can ignore a ball that is partly in the way. Concentrate on the object ball and knock it in with the tip of the cue, driving your cue straight through the cueball and the interfering ball. That's how it's presented in Herrmann and Caras. At the top of the diagram, I've added another ball. To make the nine, hit it with the eight; the cueball and thirteen get out of the way as you follow through. Shot with authority, the illegal double hit is hard to see. In the lower part of the diagram, the object is to make the ten. Bunch the balls as closely as possible and shorten your bridge to avoid an uncomfortably long cue extension. The shot is for amusement only and is not to be used as a gambling device.

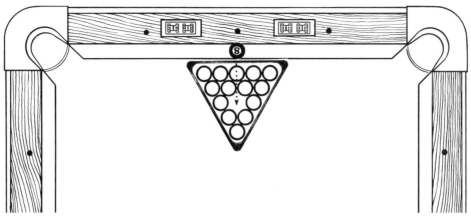

The rail bounce-in

More of a flourish than a shot. Drop the eight onto the rubber from a height of about six inches. Once you get the hang of it, you make the eight bounce into the rack nearly every time. This has been credited to Cueball Kelly.

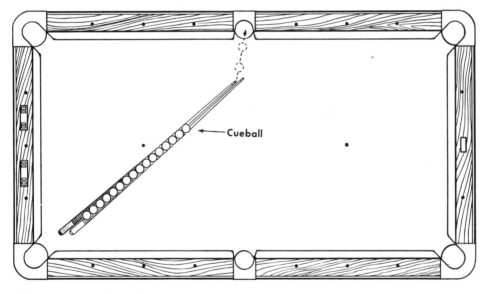

Cueball

The shunted railroad shot

Eddie Charlton is an Australian snooker champion. In his 1977 book on trick shots, mainly a rehash of Caras, is something he calls the shunting shot. Seven balls will fill a snooker pocket, but on an American pool table with gulley pockets you can use all fifteen, plus the cueball at the front as a "locomotive." Line up the balls atop the cues, with the tips offset, holding them in place with your fingers. When you have the cues oriented properly, release the cueball. Keep the cues tightly together. The balls will roll downhill one after another and make a left turn into the side pocket like a string of railroad cars being shunted onto a siding. Children laugh.

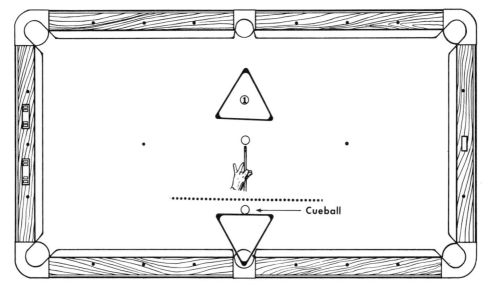

The sliding triangle

Above the dotted line, the triangle surrounds the one-ball. To make the one in the side, slam the cueball into the triangle hard enough to send the nose of the triangle into the pocket. The one will be carried forward and will drop in. Below the line, the triangle is seen as it would appear at the conclusion of the stunt. (Anonymous, 1918.)

5
Almost as Easy

Surely there were better ways of demonstrating the stability of the 1934 Studebaker.
(Billiard Archives)

To gain command over the shots described in the following fourteen diagrams requires a bit more skill and practice than for those in the previous chapter. Take care to set the balls up accurately and the same way each time the shot is tried, keeping in mind that since balls, cloth, and rubber differ from table to table and from day to day, adjustments may have to be made.

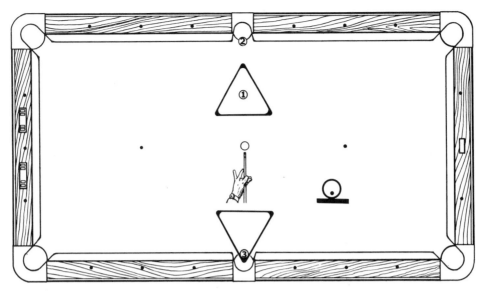

The two-triangle slide-draw

Paul Gerni showed me this one. It might be within your powers even if you have trouble drawing a ball. In the diagram, the three-ball is hanging over the lip, restrained from dropping by the corner of the triangle, which is on top of it. The slightest nudge will let the three drop. The idea is to make all three balls. Shoot hard into the triangle with draw. The front corner of the triangle knocks the two in and slides forward into the pocket (see page 58) so the one can drop. Meanwhile, the cueball backs up and hits the other triangle to dislodge the three.

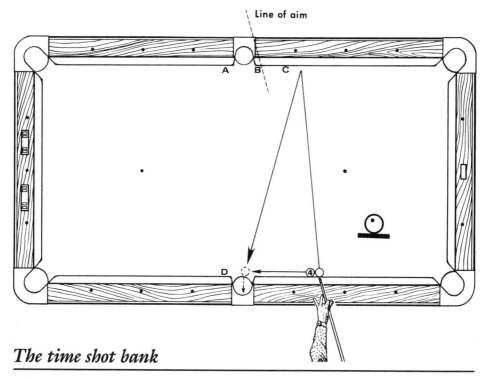

The time shot bank

The cueball is frozen to the four. The object is to make the four in the near side. Pick out an arbitrary point, B, and aim at it with left English. If the cueball returns to the near rail before the four reaches the side pocket, move B to the left; if the four arrives first, move B to the right. Once B is properly located, you have only to find the correct amount of English. B doesn't change no matter where the balls are placed. Shooting hard makes the best impression. The shot is from Anonymous, 1918; the analysis is from Jewett, 1981.

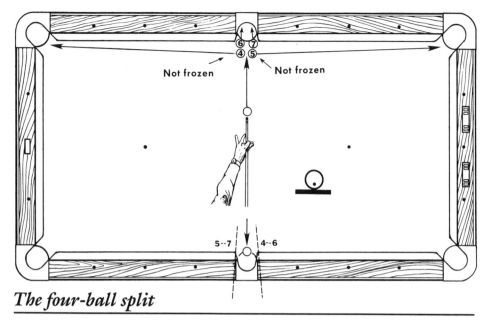

The four-ball split

Learn how to set up the cluster and you've got an easy four-ball shot. Mike Massey, the inventor, recommends not freezing the balls. An attractive option is to draw the cueball into a ball at the other side pocket, as shown in the diagram.

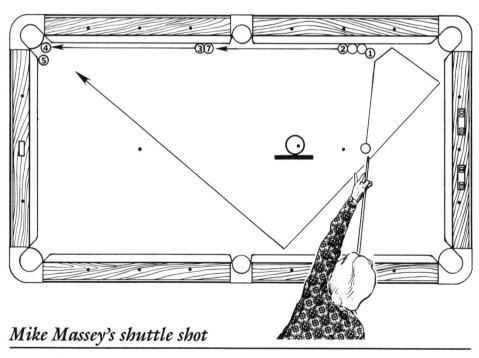

Mike Massey's shuttle shot

One of the many inventions of the man called Tennessee Tarzan. A nice feature is that after the two hits the seven and the three knocks in the four, the five holds the three in position to be pocketed by the cueball.

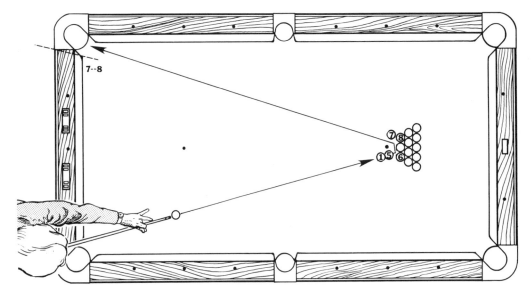

The U-turn handkerchief shot

Caras calls this the U-turn shot; Mosconi, the handkerchief shot; hence, the U-turn handkerchief shot. Covering the balls with a cloth adds dash. With the balls hidden, nobody will be able to imagine how the five emerges on the proper course. A few trial runs will reveal how best to align the seven-eight combination.

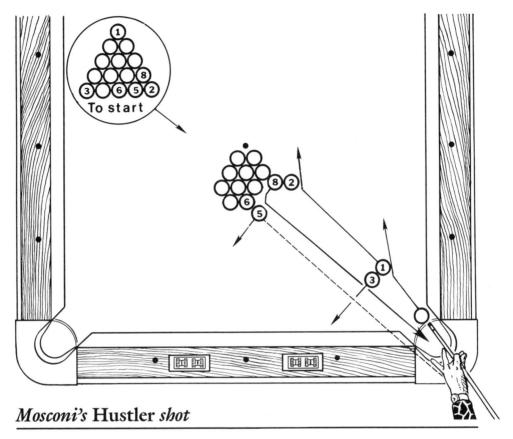

Mosconi's Hustler *shot*

In *Winning Pocket Billiards,* Willie Mosconi says that this is the shot he set up for Jackie Gleason to make in the movie *The Hustler.* Hard to guess that the eight-ball is the one that goes. Omit the one and the three until you learn the arrangement. The inset shows how to start from a full rack. Shoot hard.

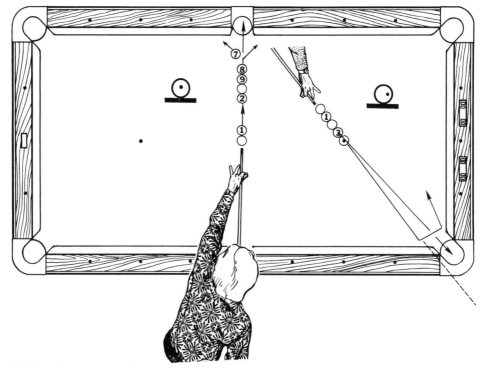

Why don't you shove it?

At the center, if you shoot the one with the cueball so that they both hit the two together, the nine will go in the side. The eight and seven are knocked aside. At the right, align the five balls as straight as you can so that they are aimed at the dashed line. Push straight ahead with maximum right English. With luck the ball at the end will not go in and the second one, the three-ball, will. Use a short bridge, as indicated, which makes it easier to follow straight through despite the resistance of the balls. Not a high-percentage shot, but mystifying when it works. (From Anonymous, 1918.)

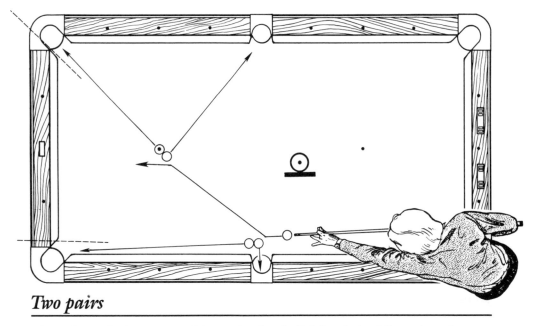

Two pairs

This takes a fairly accurate hit on the first ball. The dashed lines show how to align the combinations. (Anonymous.)

Bruce Venzke's fruit salad

Bruce Venzke, beloved columnist for the *National Billiard News,* thought of this one afternoon when he wasn't hungry. Needed is an apple tapered in the manner of a red delicious that will describe an arc when rolled on the table. A few tries will show how it should be oriented at the start. Audiences love stuff like this.

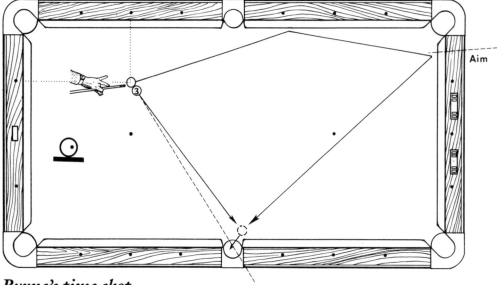

Byrne's time shot

One of the nice things about going to the trouble of writing a book is that you can include your own concoctions and name them after yourself, a prerogative I am trying to exercise with restraint. Freeze the three to the cueball and aim it at the center of the side pocket. Use the same amount of English and speed each time. Vary the line of aim until you find the point that results in the three getting knocked into the side by means of what French billiardists call a rendezvous.

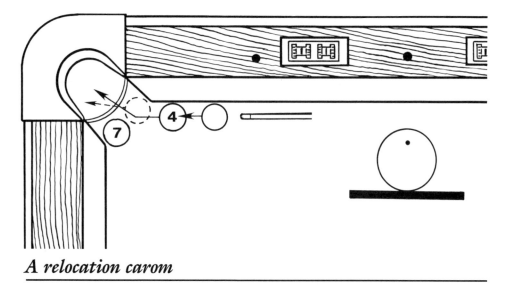

A relocation carom

Another species of rendezvous, also of my own devising. From the given position, the challenge is to make both the four and the seven. The four hits the seven on the way in, bringing the seven into position to be made by the following cueball. Doesn't work with narrow pockets.

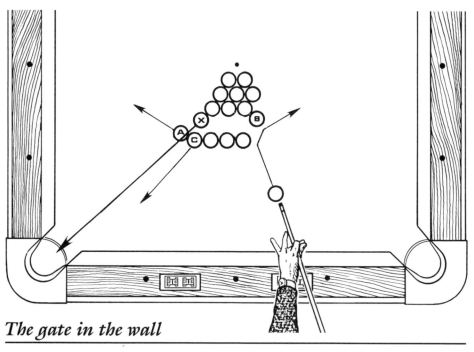

The gate in the wall

Compare this with the behind-the-wall shot in Caras, page 66. I've used his lettering so you can easily see the difference. Set up as shown above, the A and C balls split to pass the X ball.

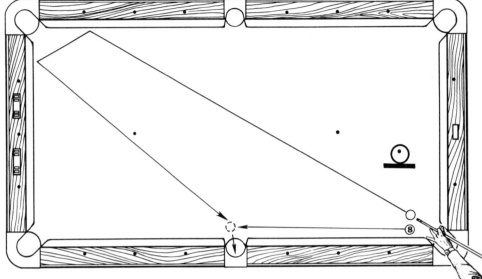

Rotten Rodney's improvement

Rotten Rodney's is the pool room Bruce Venzke co-owns in Madison, Wisconsin, hard by the university. This is his excellent improvement on the two-stroke time shot that Caras describes on page 65 of his booklet. Shoot the cueball first, *then* the eight. (The idea is to make the eight in the side.) With plenty of time to line up the two-rail cueball bank, both balls can be struck harder than in the original version with the same chance of success.

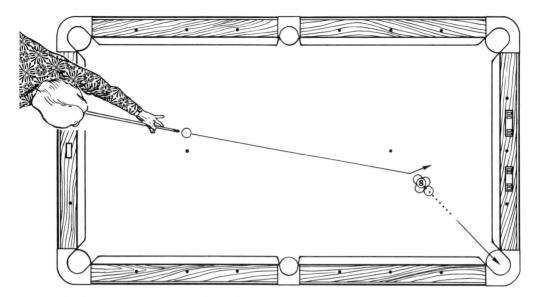

A shot from Pierre Morin

Canada is a snooker-playing country, but in Montreal there is a vigorous community of pool players. One of them is attorney Pierre Morin, who also teaches, promotes, and writes about the game. Here's an attractive idea from his *100 Trucs de Billard* (*100 Pool Trick Shots,* 1982), a collection of shots that don't require great skill. Freeze three balls together and put the eight-ball on top, forming a pyramid. Add a fourth ball to the base of the pyramid. (With clean balls on a new cloth, you'll have to use paper matches to keep the balls in place.) Shoot as shown and the eight will hop into the pocket; a hard stroke might make it go on the fly. For Pierre's book, which is in French, send $8.50 to *Les Editions de l'Homme,* 955 Amherst Street, Montreal 132, Province of Quebec, Canada H2L 3K4.

6

..., Puzzles, and ...usters

It is perhaps best to bar dogs from poolhalls entirely.
(Moldenhauer Collection)

Many trick shots are of the "So what?" variety if you simply set them up and shoot them. To be entertaining, they must be "presented." You must set the stage, lead up to a climax, make clear your intentions. Using the shot to illustrate a point or dramatize a story is good. With the right showmanship and patter, what looks drab in a diagram might be something the spectators will talk about later. An approach that works with a *small group* is to present certain shots as challenges or puzzles. Set it up, explain what is to be accomplished, and hand the cueball to somebody. Ask him or her where the cueball must be placed to reach the stated goals. Suddenly what seemed to be a dreary and meaningless bunch of pool balls becomes as intriguing as a chess problem. The shots in this chapter are particularly well suited to the puzzle treatment.

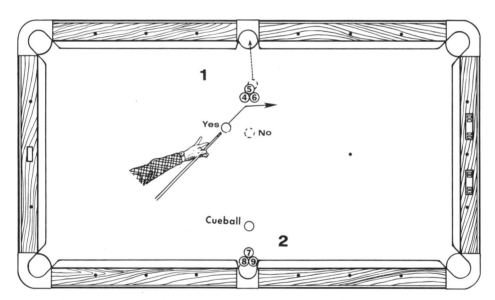

Two three-ball challenges

Can the five-ball in shot number one be made in the side? It's very unlikely from the position of the dashed ball because it's hard to hit two balls simultaneously. The best chance is to move the cueball to one side and hit the four thin, which moves the five ahead slightly to be knocked in by the six. When I say thin, I mean *thin*. In several older books, the point is made that if a match or nail is standing in the middle of three frozen balls, it can't be knocked down by the cueball. Shot two is my application of the theme. The eight and nine are hanging on the lip. Can all three balls be made in the side? No. Rich Hawkins of Kansas City did it once and is still trying to do it again.

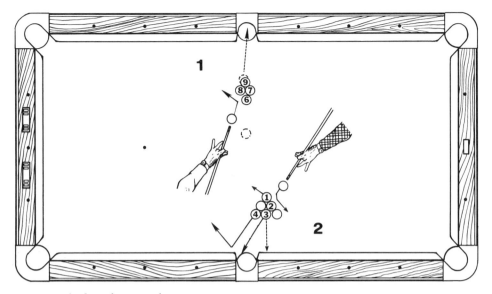

Two original puzzles

In shot one, can the nine be made? (Note gap between the eight and six.) Not from the position of the dashed circle. Use the relocation idea from the previous diagram. In shot 2, the challenge is to make the three. It's easy if you carom into the two from the one. If you hit the two first, the three will go straight to the rail.

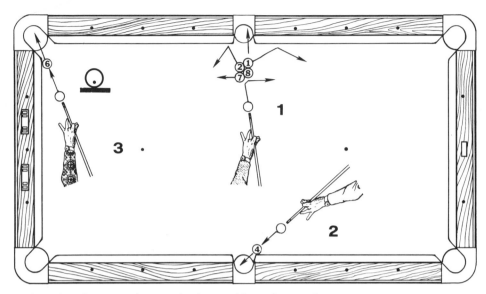

The classic stymie and the rail as interference

Shot one shows the classic four-ball stymie position from Anonymous. The idea is to make only the eight-ball. To do it, cut the seven away from the eight and then carom into it after the two and one have left. Shoot hard without aiming; to newcomers it will be inexplicable. In shot two, the four can be forced with a hard stroke through the rubber point of the pocket. It looks impossible. A lesser-known variation is shot three. Shoot straight at the six with draw and it can be forced directly into the pocket through the rubber corner of the rail. To prove that the six goes straight in, tape a friend's watch to the opposite side of the pocket jaw. If the watch gets smashed, the thesis is disproven.

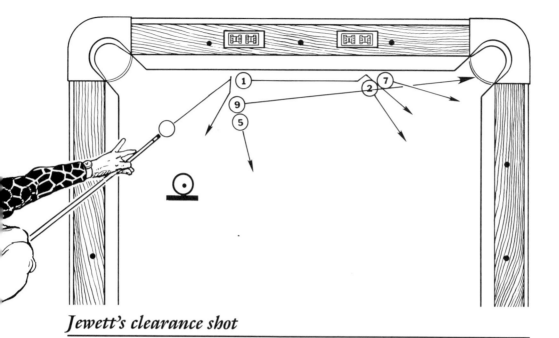

Jewett's clearance shot

You are playing nine-ball. Can you win the game in one shot? Bob Jewett shows how.

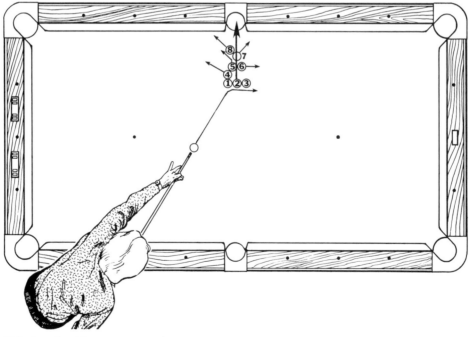

Eight-ball mystery shot

How can the two-ball be made? That is the mystery. Hit the one almost full and carom the cueball into the two. The path will be clear. (Original.)

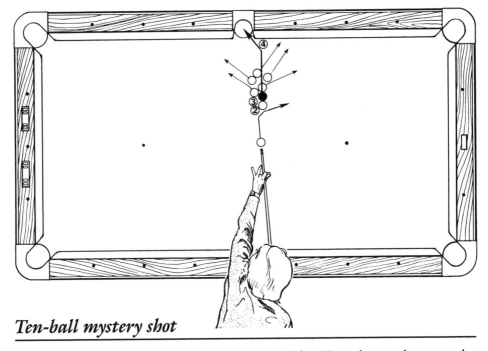

Ten-ball mystery shot

Who would guess that the black goes in the side? Note the gap between the black and the three. Precision placement is essential. (Original.)

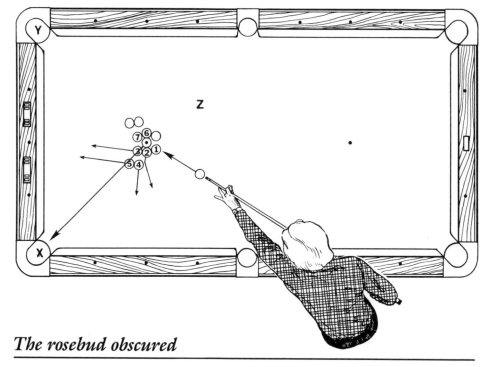

The rosebud obscured

The rosebud cluster (see page 6) can be set up with interference balls guarding the path to the corner pockets, as shown here. In the diagram, the spot ball goes in pocket X. With the cueball at Z, the spot ball goes in pocket Y. If you don't care to preserve the flexibility of being able to make the spot ball in the side pockets as well, then the nonessential balls can be placed in a random fashion so that the rosebud theme is better hidden from those who know it. (See also Varner, page 116.)

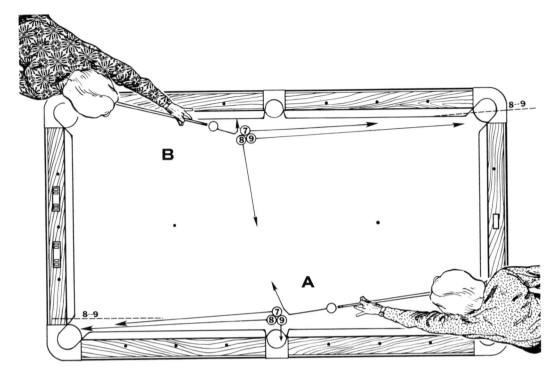

Two more three-ball challenges

Shot two on page 74 shows three balls that can't all be made. Move them away from the pocket a little, as in A, and they can be, though not in the same pocket. Shot B is a variation. In both cases the seven-ball is made by means of a carom.

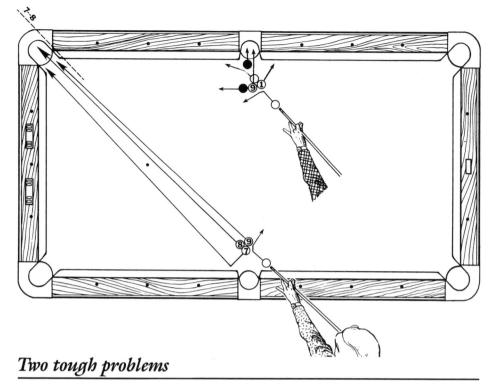

Two tough problems

At the top of the diagram, the goal is to make the nine in the side. Something like this is what I think Michael Fragale had in mind in the *National Billiard News,* December 1974. Few people could figure out how to make all the balls in the three-ball cluster at the bottom of the diagram. The shot was shown to me by Richie Ambrose.

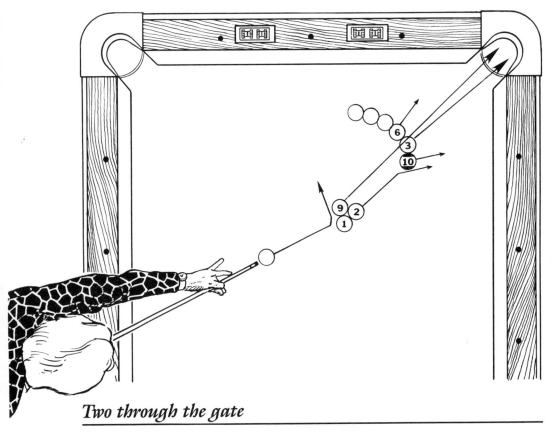

Two through the gate

Joe Procita, I learned from Jess Meshanic, was shooting this before World War II. The three goes into the pocket first and the nine follows after. Set it up so the two hits the ten and moves out of the way. (See also Caras, page 37; there only one ball goes.)

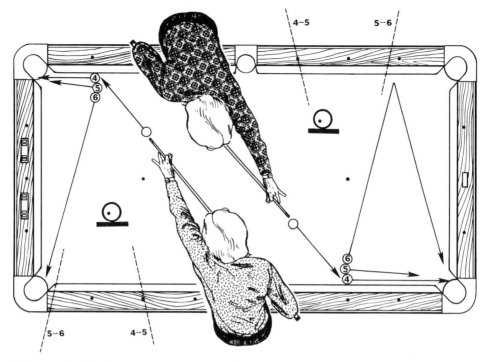

Three balls in sequence

Making three balls in numerical order from the position drawn at the left, above, is standard practice. The shot at the right, which features all three going into the same pocket, is nicer but harder. In both cases the cueball hits the four first and rebounds into the five.

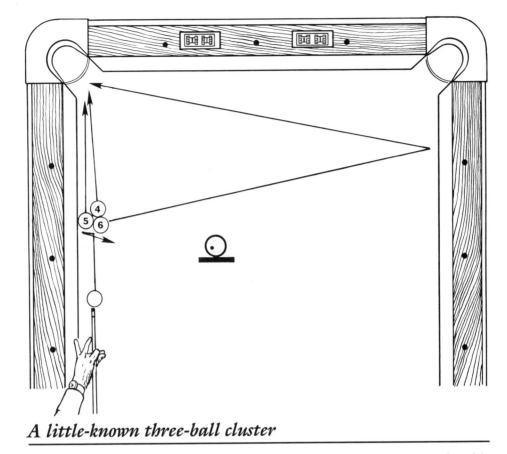

A little-known three-ball cluster

Some precision fussing will be needed to find the exact position for this three-ball shot, from Anonymous.

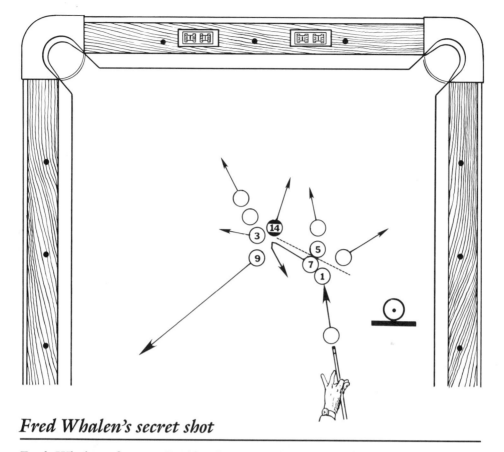

Fred Whalen's secret shot

Fred Whalen, former Pacific Coast pool champion who is now in his eighties—he looks twenty years younger—has several shots the secrets of which only he knows. I talked him into explaining one for this book. In the diagram, the dashed line is the kiss line between the seven and the five. The seven is aimed so it hits the fourteen first, then the three, then the nine. For maximum effect, put the cueball at the other end of the table and ask anybody which ball will go. Fred forces his victim to name a ball. The nine is never named, because he starts with a ball blocking its path to the side pocket. If, say, the five is named, he takes the ball blocking the nine and moves it next to the five. "Wrong," he says, pulling the trigger, "the nine in the side." Even without the preliminary byplay, it's hard to see how the nine will go in the side, certainly not with the uncanny accuracy Fred brings to the shot. In setting it up, put the nine on the spot. The gap between the three and nine, which is crucial, is approximately an inch.

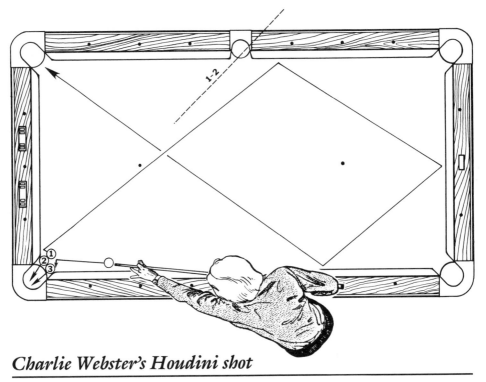

Charlie Webster's Houdini shot

Charlie Webster and Irvin Allen run the "Gentlemen's Cue" in Pikesville, Maryland. One day in a game of one-pocket, Charlie was faced with a situation from which there seemed no escape. His opponent needed two more balls and had managed to herd the remaining three into the jaws of his pocket. Charlie needed to make one ball in the other corner pocket. His amazing solution is diagrammed. He made his opponent's two balls, but he made his own as well, four rails, to win the game. Now it's one of his favorite trick shots; for him it's high percentage. Aim the one-two combo at the side pocket as shown. Hit the one-ball half full with slight left English. Nice shot, Charlie.

7
Novelty Shots

As E. A. Hungerford said in *A Practical Primer on Billiards*
(Brunswick-Balke-Collender, circa 1916): "The YMCA billiard room under a strong
Christian man will get many into Bible classes and Church membership."
(Moldenhauer Collection)

By novelty shots I mean those using props of some kind: triangles, pieces of chalk, the rake, ball trays, tennis balls, or whatever. Introducing things of this kind into an exhibition program adds color and interest, and this chapter, which presents a dozen or so of my favorites, only scratches the surface of what could be invented. Cueball Kelly substitutes a golf ball for the cueball to make several shots that would otherwise be impossible; a golf ball bounces backward off the object ball with such alacrity it doesn't create the double-kiss problem a ball of normal weight would. Perhaps a bowling ball or a shot put could be used with comic effect to smash through interfering balls. Let me know if you come up with anything interesting.

What Stonik did was run 46 in straight pool on a pool table. Lou Butera, who has run over 100 the same way, learned his one-handed skills from Stonik himself.

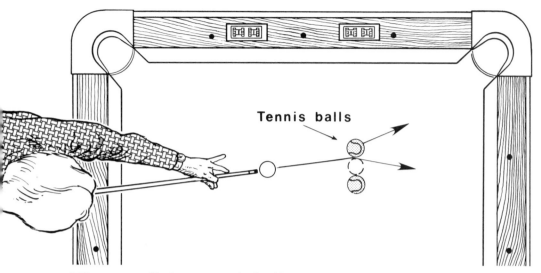

The tantalizing tennis balls

Herrmann mentions an impossible carom using two corks and a cueball. Tennis balls, which perhaps were scarcer than corks in 1902, are better. Place the tennis balls so that a cueball can just barely pass between them. In the diagrammed position, try to carom the cueball from one tennis ball to other. Certain insufferable know-it-alls will bet they can do it. They will lose.

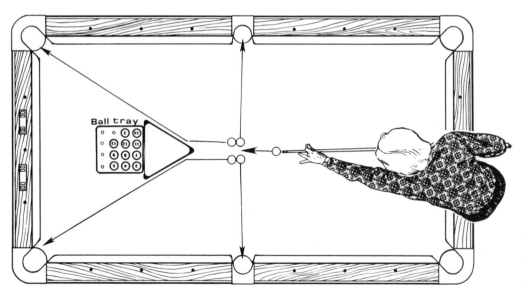

The fork in the road

When faced with a fork in the road, try going in all directions, including sideways. The tray is needed to keep the triangle from being knocked out of line by the forward balls, one of which is almost bound to hit it first. (Original.)

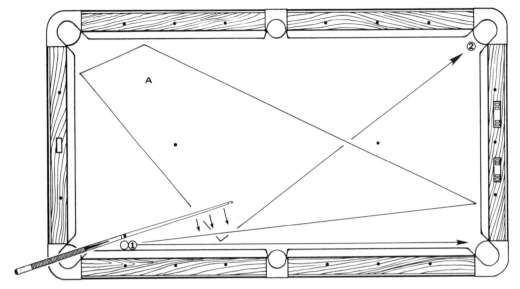

The pool sweep

The idea of sweeping a ball down the rail, imparting both speed and spin, goes back to Herrmann. The above elaboration was diagrammed for me by Jim Rempe. The cueball and the one-ball are frozen on the rail. Using a friend's cue that you wouldn't mind breaking, press it against the side of the cueball hard enough to make both balls move forward. Move the cue in the direction of the short arrows. The balls will squirt down the table because of the squeezing action. The idea is to send the one directly into the corner pocket and the cueball off five rails to make the two. Charles Cook, affectionately known in the trade as Bucktooth, showed me another version. Start with the two-ball at A. After the cueball is in motion, hit the two slowly toward the upper right pocket so that it arrives just in time to be knocked in by the cueball. That's showmanship, folks.

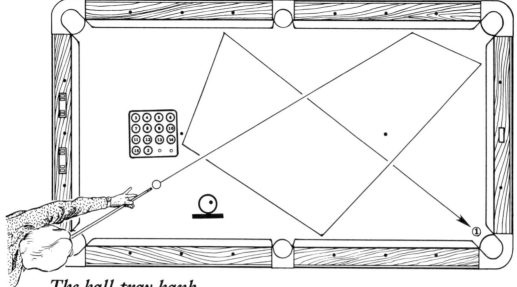

The ball-tray bank

Before dismantling your cue and slipping into the night (I assume you know enough to demand payment in advance), show the awestruck assemblage just one more. Put the ball tray on the table at the spot or a few inches above it. (Exactly where depends on its shape and health. It must be plastic with a curled edge.) A cueball banked three rails will come off the front of the tray with enough spin to carry it to the vicinity of the lower right corner pocket, where the one is waiting.

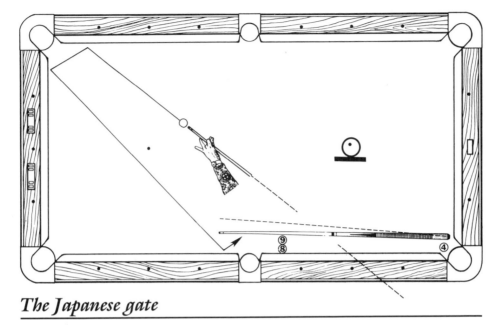

The Japanese gate

Noriko Katsura of Tokyo, one of the fabulous billiard-playing Katsura sisters, showed me this one when she was in California in the mid-1970s. State that you will make the four without jumping over the cue, knocking the cue into the four, or touching the nine and eight. The charming solution is diagrammed. The cue swings out of the way and guides the cueball around the nine and eight to the four. It takes practice, but not much.

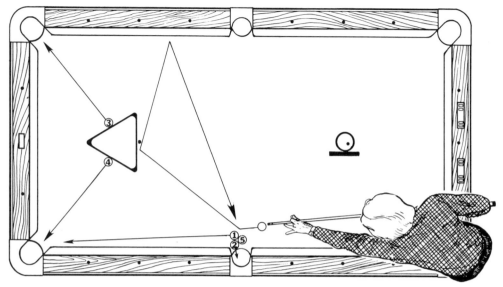

Five-ball triangle shot

Hit the one with low right. The one sinks the two and goes on to drop in the corner. The cueball hits the center of the triangle, making the three and four, then returns off the upper rail to make the five. (Original.)

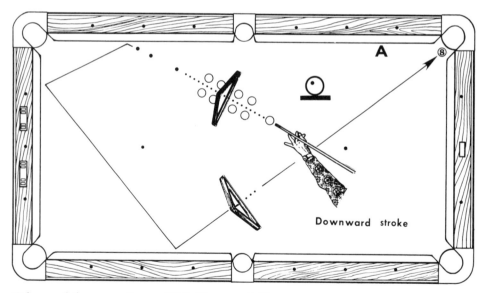

Downward stroke

The golden arches of Hollywood Fats

A fairly easy crowd-pleaser from Harry "Hollywood Fats" Sims, the 1980 national three-cushion champion. Elevate your cue and jump the cueball through the first upright triangle and over the obstacle balls. Coming off the third rail, the cueball strikes the bottom of the second upright triangle, jumps in the air again, and continues to pocket the eight. The shot is almost a cinch if a cue is laid along the rail at A to guide a cueball that comes in too short.

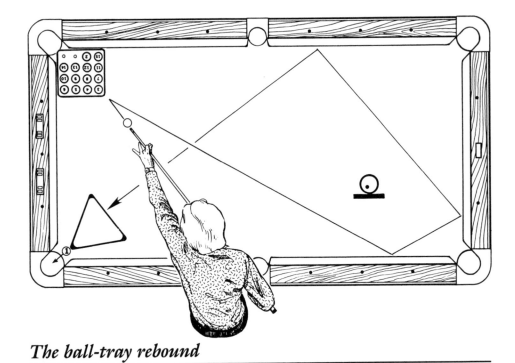

The ball-tray rebound

Wedge the tray in the corner and draw off the corner with a hard stroke using low left English. Be sure a ball is in the tray at the corner the cueball strikes. Using a triangle to enlarge the margin of error is not my idea, but the rest of the shot is.

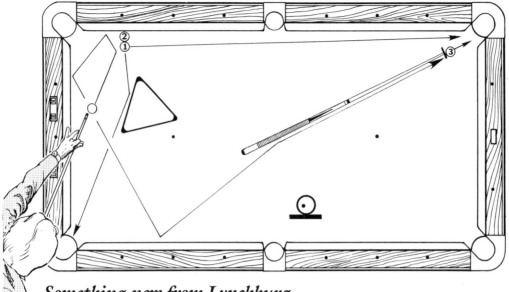

Something new from Lynchburg

A tip of the hat to Bill Marshall for something definitely different. The one kisses off the two into the corner, the two banks into the triangle and caroms into a pocket, the cueball hits the side of the rake, and is guided down the shaft to the head to bump the three into the corner.

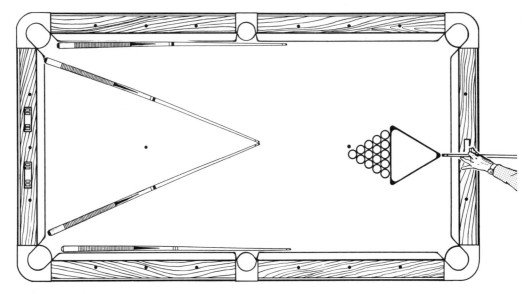

The wild stampede of Tony Meatballs

Tony Meatballs is a veteran practitioner of pool who plays at Al Balukas's Bay Ridge Billiards in Brooklyn. This is his shot, according to Pete Margo. Gulley pockets are needed. Line up the racked balls off center so the lead ball won't hit the central cuetips squarely. Place four guide cues as shown. The idea is to send all the balls rushing down the table and into the left corner pockets. Sometimes almost all of them will drop. A crazy idea that always brings smiles.

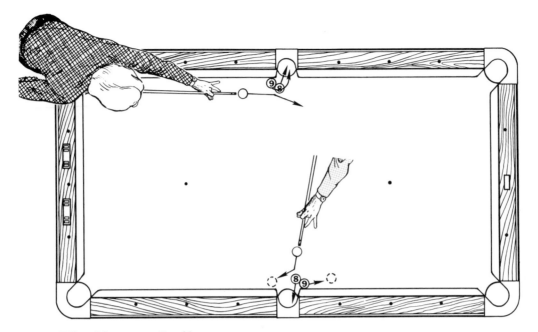

The Siamese Balls

Ask a member of the audience who knows the game how he would handle the situation at the bottom of the diagram. The game is rotation or nine-ball. If he proceeds as shown, caroming the eight lightly off the nine to bring the nine off the rail for an easy corner shot, he gets high marks. Show him how you would do it by setting them up again (top), but this time you secretly switch in two balls that are permanently joined by a double-threaded screw. Hit the eight hard and the nine-ball will swing around faster than the eye can follow and go into the pocket too. Jaws will drop onto chests all over the Hippodrome. (Origin unknown.)

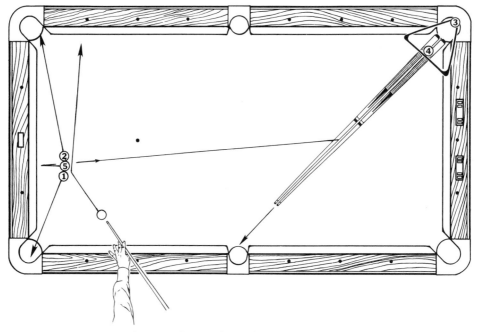

Novelty railroad switchyard

The three-ball is precariously resting on a piece of chalk so that the slightest nudge will topple it into the pocket. The five-ball jumps the cues, rides uphill to hit the triangle, thus making the four and three, then rolls back down the cues into the side pocket. (From Bill Marshall.)

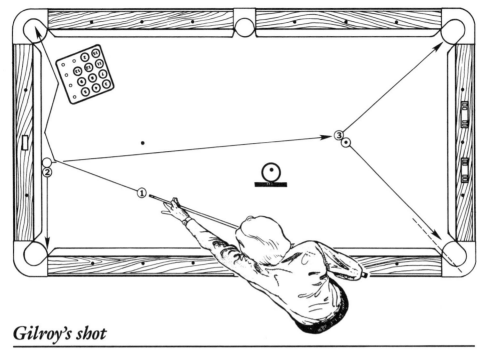

Gilroy's shot

Call the police in Gilroy, California, and you might learn this shot, which was invented by Kim Merrill, a straight-shooting officer of the law in that city, also known as the Garlic Capital of the World. Experimentation is required to find the exact spot to put the cueball and the two. While searching for it, put the one at the same place every time and use a half-ball hit on the cueball. If all goes well, the cueball will be the only ball left on the table. The annual Garlic Festival is held in August.

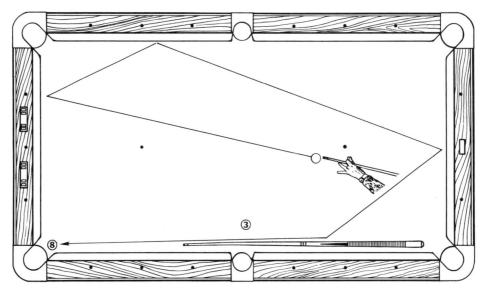

Shooting on cue

Audiences respond well to gags like this if the rest of your show is legitimate. Without the cue on the table, announce that you will bank the cueball around the table (indicate the path approximately) and go through the space between the side pocket and the three, without touching the three, to make the eight. The shot is impossible without cheating, which you do by laying your cue on the table as shown after the cueball is in motion. (Contributed by Victor Maduro of the Republic of Panama.)

8
Tube Shots

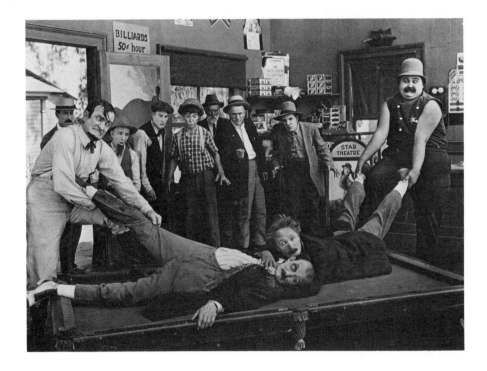

If there is a waiting list, poolhall etiquette dictates that players relinquish the table after a reasonable time.
(Moldenhauer Collection)

Almost all of the shots in this chapter are new, and by new I mean 1981. Except for those in the first two diagrams, I invented all of them, a spasm of creativity that made me so proud I went to a junk shop and bought a medal for my lapel. It's from the Crimean War, but who's to know? The idea of resting pool balls on top of something and shooting under them goes back at least to 1902. Herrmann describes a shot with balls placed on large kitchen match boxes. The next application I know about appears in a film made at the 1936 world three-cushion tournament; Johnny Layton is shown doing the shot diagrammed on page 242. When I showed Sax Dal Porto some of my tube shots, he remembered a simple one Charlie Peterson used to do thirty or forty years ago, which is given on the next page.

For tubes I recommend paper coin wrappers. They are available free of charge at any bank and are light enough to be knocked aside without deflecting the cueball.

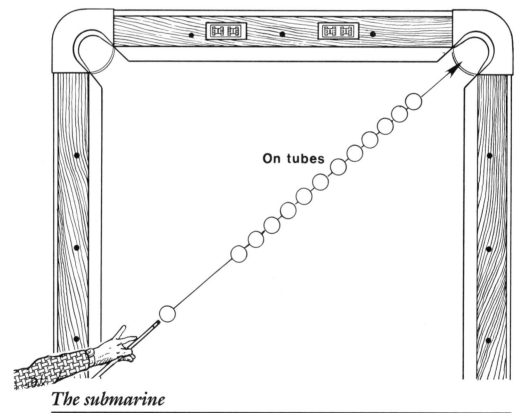

On tubes

The submarine

Put all of the object balls on tubes in a straight line and simply fire the cueball under them into a pocket. It looks good on television in slow motion, Pete Margo assures me, because the balls drop to the table and bounce, creating a wave motion. Ernie Costa uses rolled-up playing cards secured by rubber bands; heavier than coin wrappers, they make a nice explosion effect. I've never seen Ernie do it, however. In fact, I've never seen Ernie.

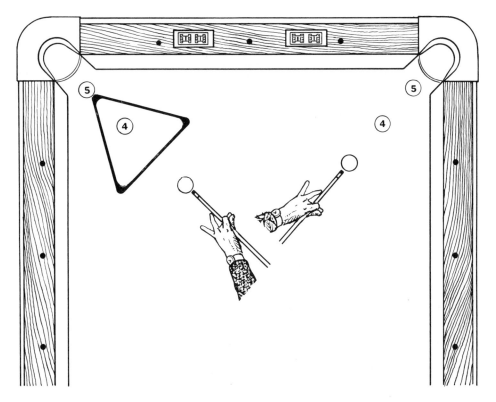

A moderately amusing sequence

The simple positions above can serve as the basis of a sequence that is both entertaining and comical, provided you are both entertaining and comical yourself. At the upper right, how can the five be made without touching the four, barring a jump shot? Charlie Peterson, according to the aforementioned Mr. Dal Porto, after a spectator gave up, put the four on a tube and shot the cueball under it. The idea can be carried further. Make the four and not the five by putting the five on a tube. Make the four and the five by putting the five on a tube and follow on the cueball. Can the five be made without touching the four if the four can't be put on a tube? Yes, by putting the cueball on a tube and shooting over the four. Finally, can the five be made without touching the four if the tubes are barred entirely? The solution is at the left of the diagram.

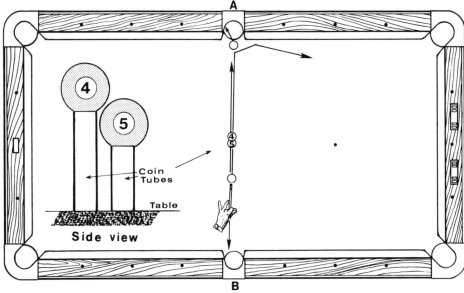

The penny wrapper overlap

Thinking up this is one of the five or six most adorable things I've ever done in my life. I began showing the shot in the spring of 1981, and by fall it had been done on television by Mike Massey and rushed into print by Pete Margo, Nick Varner, and Paul Gerni. It's new, different, easy, and it sticks in the minds of spectators; shots like that are hard to find. Take two coin wrappers and cut one to a length of exactly two and a half inches. Use them to tee up two balls in the middle of the table, one overlapping the other. Shoot the cueball under them, knocking the tubes away and pocketing a ball in the side. When the elevated balls hit the table they collide and are sent scurrying into pockets A and B in a most enjoyable manner. The cueball, of course, can be made to do something more heroic than pocket a single ball, but I feel that would detract from the charming central idea.

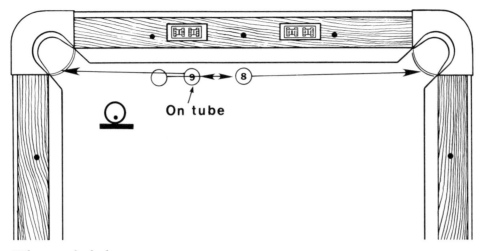

On tube

The aerial draw

Can both balls be made if the nine is on a tube? Yes, by hitting the cueball low.
After the cueball has passed underneath and the nine has dropped to the table,
the cueball draws back and hits the nine from the far side.

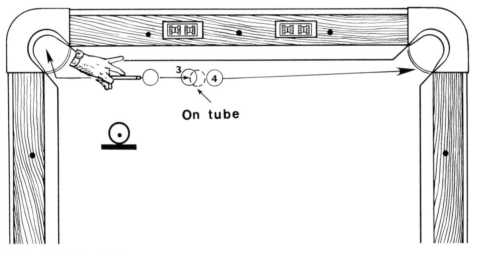

On tube

The half-ball drop

The three is tubed and the gap between it and the four, measured horizontally,
is half a ball. If you shoot under the three with stop action, it will land on the
cueball and carom into the left corner pocket.

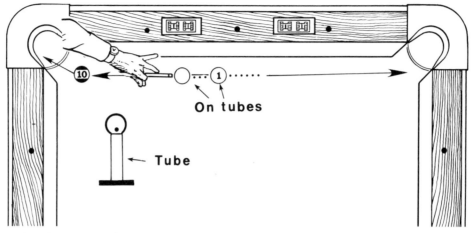

On tubes

Tube

The free-fall draw

Can backspin be put on a cueball on a tube? To the best of my knowledge, the question has never occurred to even our greatest philosophers. Once at a table, the answer soon was mine and it was yes. The inset shows draw being applied to the cueball atop the tube. The one-ball is atop a tube as well. The bridge is freehand—that is, the hand is held off the table. The cue is level. The cueball flies through the air, knocks the one off its perch into the right corner pocket, then drops to the cloth and backs up to make the 10. The action is so uncanny perhaps the question should be addressed not by philosophers but by theologians.

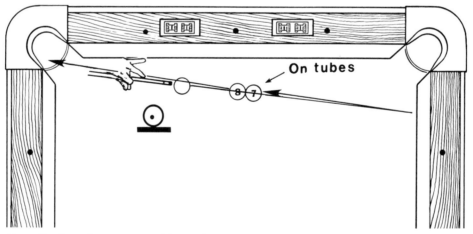

On tubes

Banked subway combination

Both object balls are on tubes and are frozen in the air on a line with the left corner pocket. When the cueball passes beneath them, you will smile attractively when you see that they stay in position after landing on the table. A touch of left English brings the cueball back to pocket the eight in the left corner pocket on a combination.

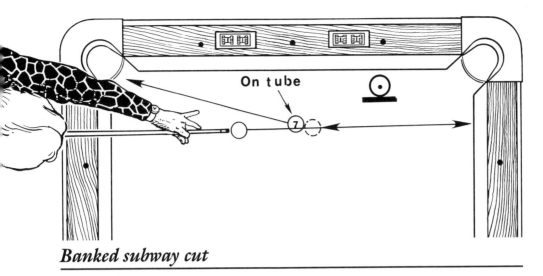

Banked subway cut

A harder version of the preceding shot using just one ball.

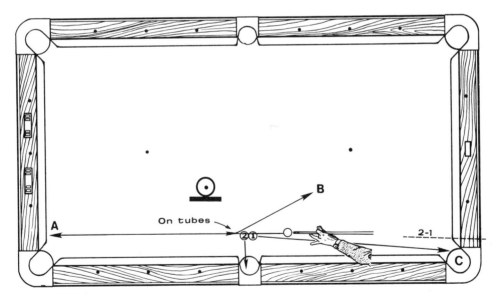

The aerial sideshow

The one and two are atop tubes, frozen together in a line parallel to the rail. The cueball is half an inch farther from the rail. If you can shoot perpendicularly into the rail at A with absolutely no English, the cueball will return to hit the outside of the two-ball, caroming off toward B. The two will go into the side and the one into the corner C. Not for beginners.

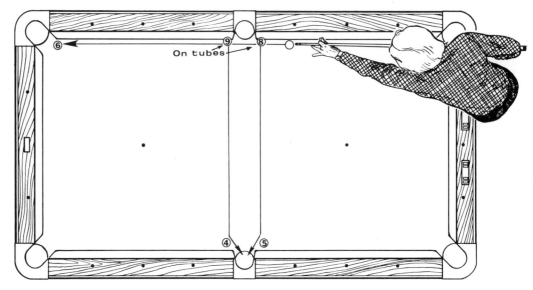

The rail nose transfer

I like this because watchers have no idea of what you are planning until you tell them. Place the eight and nine on tubes so that part of the balls overlap the nose of the cushion. Shoot under them, taking out the tubes, to pocket the six. The eight and nine will scoot straight across the table and, if you've located the bumper balls correctly, will go into the side.

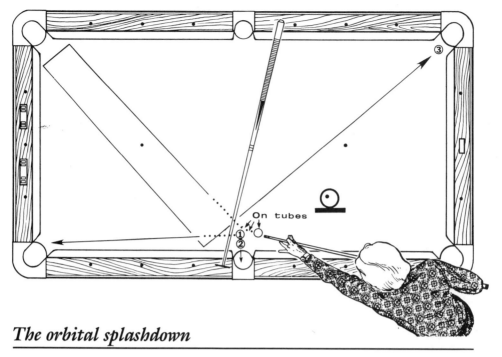

On tubes

The orbital splashdown

The cueball, the one, and the two are on tubes. The three isn't. With your
bridge hand in the air and the cue level, hit the outside of the one with high
left English. Hit enough of the one and use enough speed to get both the one
and the cueball *over* the rake. The idea is to make the cueball bank off three
rails and go under the rake to pocket the three. A showy attention getter.

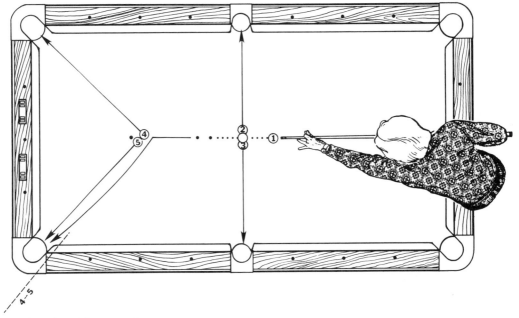

The double overlap

A coin wrapper isn't long enough for this shot. You'll have to make a tube out of paper so that the cueball is about six inches off the table. Examine the drawing and note that if the cueball drops straight down it will send both the two and the three into the side pockets. The problem is to shoot the one-ball over the two and three and under the cueball without touching any of them. You can do it with a downward jump stroke or by teeing the one up on a piece of chalk. Try to make all the numbered balls, leaving only the cueball on the table.

9

Shots with One Ball

Bouncing a ball on a cue is hard even for jugglers.
(Moldenhauer Collection)

Shots involving large clusters and full racks can be spectacular, but exhibition players tend to shun them because they take too long to set up. A sweating performer trying to hammer a dozen balky balls into precise positions is about as interesting as watching paint flake. If you intend to make large cluster shots part of your show, make sure you have some excellent jokes to tell (see Note). The virtue of the one-ball shots in this chapter is that they can be set up instantly. Many of the principles they so starkly elucidate can be made use of under game conditions.

NOTE: For readers who may not know any, here is an excellent joke, invented by Derek Knell of Tiff's North Hollywood Billiards:

Judge: What is your client charged with?
Lawyer: She's charged with beating her husband to death with a billiard cue.
Judge: How many innings?

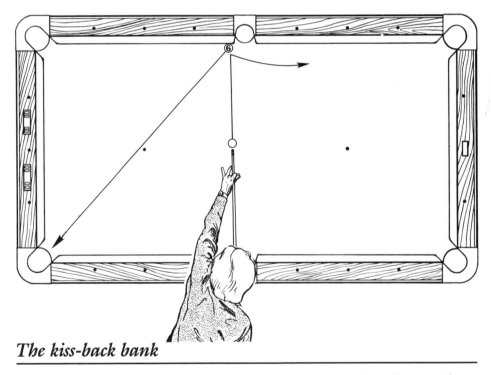

The kiss-back bank

Can the six be banked in the corner without scratching in the side? Yes, if you hit it full enough to get a double kiss. A useful idea in the game of one-pocket.

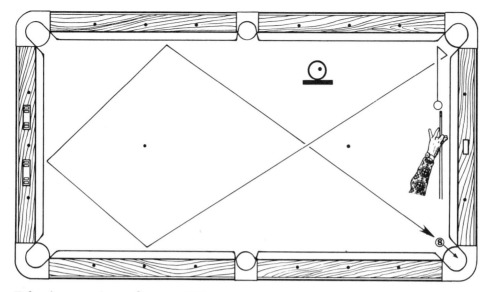

The jaw-points five-rail bank

An unusual bank shot shown to me by Bob Nicholl.

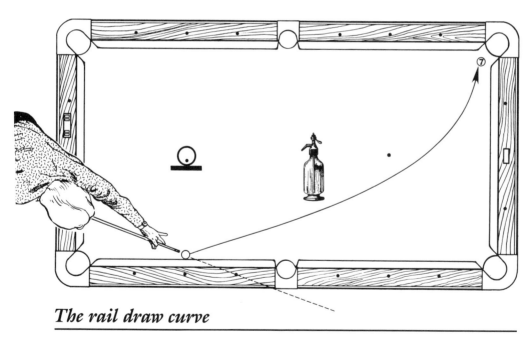

The rail draw curve

Freeze the ball on the second diamond and aim at the third diamond with extreme low draw. Properly stroked, the cueball will bend around intervening obstacles. (Also see page 122.)

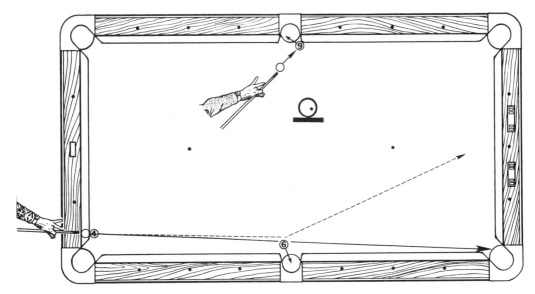

The hopscotch shot and the side-pocket squeeze

I thought I invented the shot at the top of the diagram until I saw it in Herrmann. Hit the nine softly a hair to the right of full with extreme right English. The transferred English can squeeze the nine to the left and into the pocket. At the bottom left, the cueball is on top of the rubber, propped in place by the four-ball, which is frozen to the cushion. The original version of the shot called for making both balls in the corner pocket, cueball first. (The cueball rides over the four and lands in front of it.) A more interesting idea is to use the cueball to take out an interfering ball, clearing the path for the four.

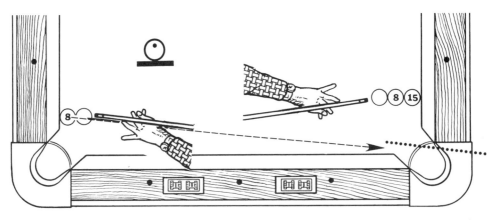

The Hustler *bank, plus*

This is the shot Paul Newman fleeced the yokels with in the movie *The Hustler*. To bank the eight, hit the cueball high and use an open bridge so the cue can ride up out of the way of the rebounding balls. Angle the cue so the butt is over the opposite corner pocket. I much prefer the version with the extra ball, as given at right, because there seems to be no way the fifteen can be banked. The same instructions apply. Both are from Anonymous, 1918.

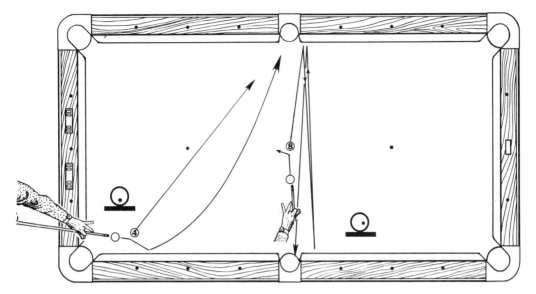

The high-road shot and the center-table triple bank

At the lower left, the four takes the low road and the cueball takes the high road. Thanks to draw, the cueball gets to the side pocket first. In the middle of the diagram, the eight-ball is on the center spot. With heavy right English, the eight triple banks in the side. Fascinating. (Shown to me by Paul Gerni.)

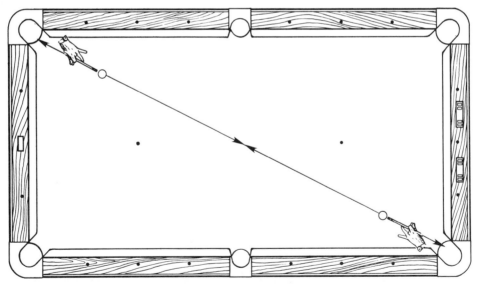

The two-man precision reaction shot

The two cueballs must be placed exactly on the line connecting the corner pockets. Two players aim at each other's ball and pull the trigger simultaneously. Soft speed is sufficient. The balls meet and rebound backward into the corner pockets. I didn't believe it either when Paul Gerni described the shot, but we made it on the third try. Legend has it that Gerni and Jim Rempe created the shot late one night in Davenport, Iowa.

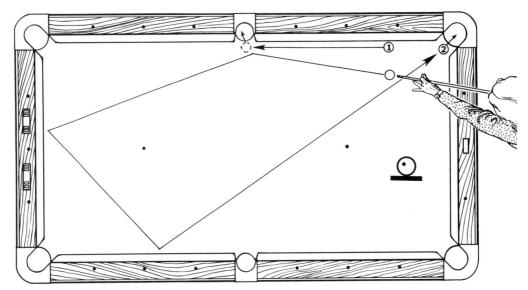

The side-pocket wing shot and beyond

Shoot the one-ball slowly along the rail, then reposition yourself behind the cueball. When the one reaches the side, fire it in. Very funny. (Well, funny.) Ivor Bransford takes the idea one step farther by going two rails to pocket another ball, as shown. Shelton, Washington, has never seen anything like Ivor.

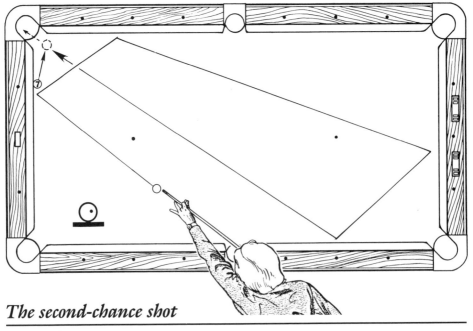

The second-chance shot

Hit the rail first, barely touching the seven-ball, which gets nudged toward the corner pocket. The cueball is supposed to go four rails to hit the seven again, pocketing it. Norm Smith, who showed me this shot, said he learned it when he was seven years old and didn't make it until he was thirty-nine.

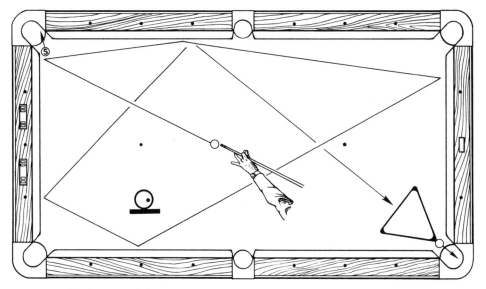

Around the world

This is my adaptation to pool of a common billiard pattern. Shoot as hard as you can and hit the rail before the five. The courageous can try to scratch in the lower right corner. The rest of us will pocket a second ball with the aid of a triangle.

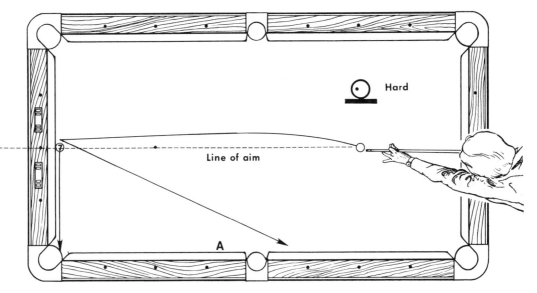

Hard

Line of aim

A

The impossible cut

The cueball is on the spot and the seven is frozen to the center of end rail. One would think, therefore, that it would be impossible to cut the seven into the corner, but one would be wrong. The secret is to hit the rail first. There must be enough English on the cueball to bring it to A if you miss the seven entirely. The aiming point depends on the spindliness of the cue; with many cues you must aim on the *left* side of the seven. Try the dashed line, then adjust the line of aim to suit your cue. Experts often show this shot with the cueball on top of the rail on the nameplate. (See also pages 120 and 264 in *Byrne's Standard Book of Pool and Billiards,* available at all decent bookstores.)

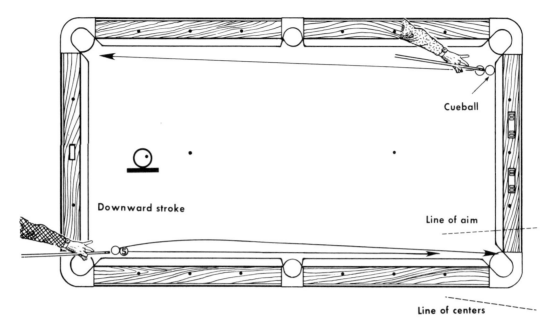

Cueball

Downward stroke

Line of aim

Line of centers

The frozen kick and the passing lane

The shot at the top is similar to *The Hustler* bank on page 114, but in this case the cueball is against the rail. To make the object ball, shoot over it into the cueball. In the hands of Steve Mizerak, the object ball goes into the left corner pocket at ninety miles an hour. The shot is usually set up across the width of the table rather than the length. Ivor Bransford does it that way, sending the cueball off the far end rail to make a ball in the side as well. The shot at the bottom is fascinating. By shooting downward on the cueball, it can be made to pass the five-ball and beat it into the corner pocket. George Middleditch invented this and makes it a feature of his act. Plenty of high right English is required. Elevate about forty-five degrees.

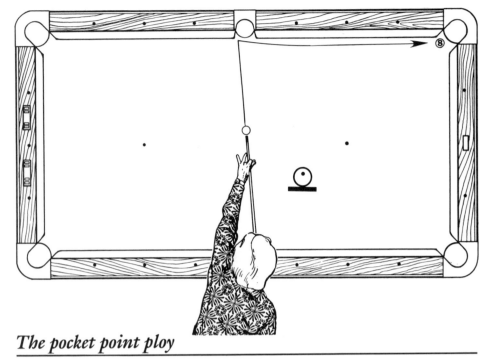

The pocket point ploy

Going off the point of the side pocket is sometimes the best way to escape interfering balls, and it can be done from far to the left or right. Only imaginative shotmakers like California's Cole Dickson think of it in games. I leave it to the reader to create a trick shot making use of the idea.

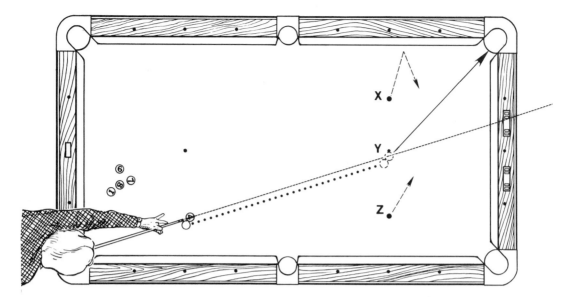

Winging it

Good players can throw a ball down the table and cut it in the corner while it's on the move. Great players like Don Willis can do it with billiard balls on a snooker table. Bob Jewett's half-ball approach makes the so-called wing shot a bit easier than it looks. Shoot or throw the four toward the spot along the dashed line. Shoot the cueball along the dotted line, timing it so contact is made near the spot. The advantage is that there is something to aim at, namely, half of the object ball. For something harder, cut the object ball from Z or bank it from X. Kim Merrill banks his wing shots four rails. The anonymous author of *Trick and Fancy Pocket Billiard Shots* suggests throwing *both* the object ball and the cueball down the table and cutting one in with the other while both are on the move. Those old-timers must have been fast on their feet.

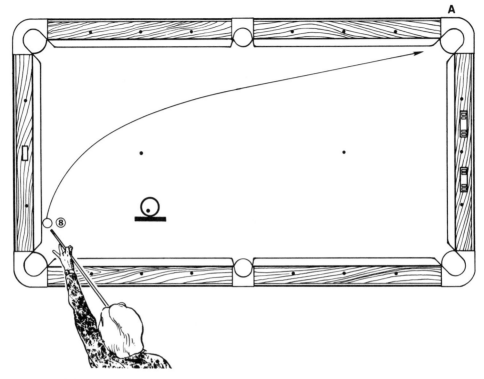

A good but not great escape

The cueball is frozen to the rail behind the eight. With draw and a touch of left the cueball can be made to curve into pocket A, or perhaps make a ball jawed there. This strikes me as a more effective demonstration of the principle used in the better-known shot on page 113. (From Victor Maduro.)

10
Jump Shots

Willie Hoppe prepares to knock a ball off Buster Keaton's hat. A miscue
would have changed the course of movie history.

One of the reasons teachers tell students to keep their cues level, even on draw shots, is that when you elevate the butt of the cue even a little and strike the cueball a downward blow, the cueball leaves the cloth. It's amazing how many people don't know this simple fact, which has been around for centuries. There are times, of course, when you *want* the cueball to become airborne, such as when you are trying to make the shots in this chapter. The altitude the cueball attains and the length of the flight depends on the elevation of the cue and the speed of the takeoff. Practice will enable you to acquire the necessary touch. Finding sufficient practice time in what you think is a busy day is all a matter of priorities. Tougher to solve is the problem of poolroom proprietors, who tend to become livid at the sight of people practicing jump shots. Coping with proprietors is beyond the scope of this book. Try stealth.

Ripley's——Believe It or Not!®

INTENDED SHOT

FLOOR

WHEN BILL BELL TRIED TO MAKE A SIDE POCKET SHOT
AT POCKET BILLIARDS - THE BALL JUMPED THE TABLE
BOUNCED OFF THE FLOOR TO THE NEXT TABLE - AND
EXECUTED THE IDENTICAL SHOT
HE WAS TRYING TO MAKE ON THE
FIRST TABLE! Salvation Army
Service Men's Club
Boston

© RIPLEY INTERNATIONAL LIMITED 1945

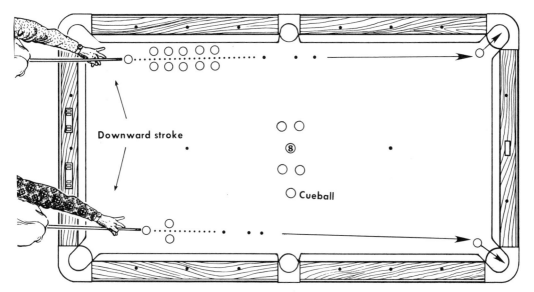

Downward stroke

Cueball

The squeeze-through jump

At the lower left are two balls a ball-width apart. You can impress the uninformed with your incredible accuracy by shooting between them, touching neither, and pocketing a ball in the corner as well, if you will raise the back of your cue slightly. That the cueball *jumps* through the gap is imperceptible. This was a common hustling trick a hundred years ago, according to *Billiards Made Easy,* published in London in 1880. A nice variation is given by Anonymous, and is rendered at the center. The cueball jumps through the first pair and the eight jumps through the next pair of interfering balls, the eight ending up in the side pocket. To "squeeze through" a whole corridor of balls, as at the top of the diagram, takes more elevation of the cue butt and more power.

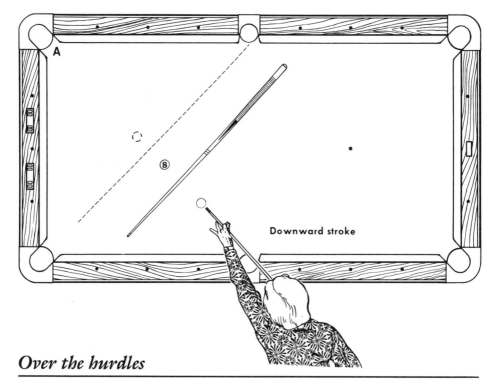

Downward stroke

Over the hurdles

What if your ill-mannered opponent tries to stop you from making the eight in pocket A by laying his cue on the table? No problem. Use a downward stroke and the cueball will clear the cue with ease. A second cue (dashed line) makes no difference, because the eight, having been struck from above by the cueball, will leap over it. Even a ball in the way (dashed circle) can be hurdled by the eight if the cueball strikes the eight from a high enough angle. For players like Steve Mizerak and Machine Gun Lou Butera, these are very high-percentage shots.

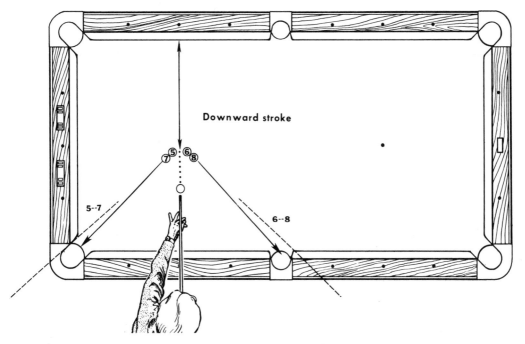

A backward double combination

Set up this cluster and see if anybody can figure out how to make the seven and eight. The method is to jump over the gap and hit the five and six on the way back. (Original.)

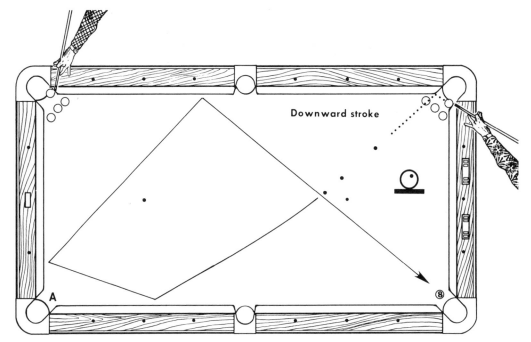

Two corner jumps

At the upper right, the cueball is trapped behind a wall of balls. In 1827, Captain Mingaud showed how the cueball could escape by jumping it off the point of the pocket with a sharp, downward stroke. He used to pocket a ball at A. Jim Rempe showed me the diagrammed pattern, which requires right English. The eight can also be made from the upper left corner by shooting a jump shot off the short-rail pocket point.

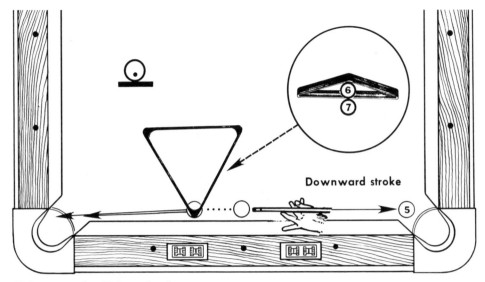

The two-ball stack shot

I'd like to know who invented this. Put one ball atop another and hold them in place by resting the corner of a triangle on them. By using low draw and a downward stroke, not only can both balls be made in the left corner pocket, the cueball will back up to make the five.

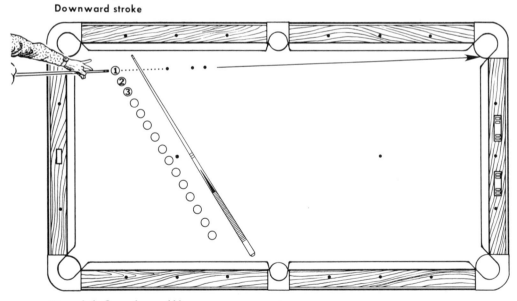

Rapid-fire hurdling

Jean Balukas, who wins the world's women's pool title whenever she wants to and whose high run in straight pool is 134, makes a memorable show out of this shot. The idea is to jump the balls in sequence over the cue and into the corner pocket, moving quickly from one to another. She does it at bewildering speed. Audiences are more easily aroused by this sort of thing than by more technical skill shots.

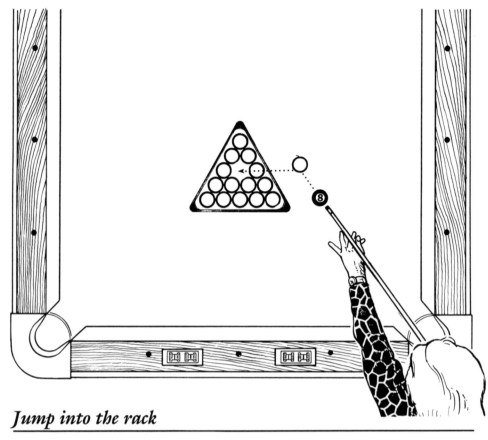

Jump into the rack

Everybody else does it, why not you?

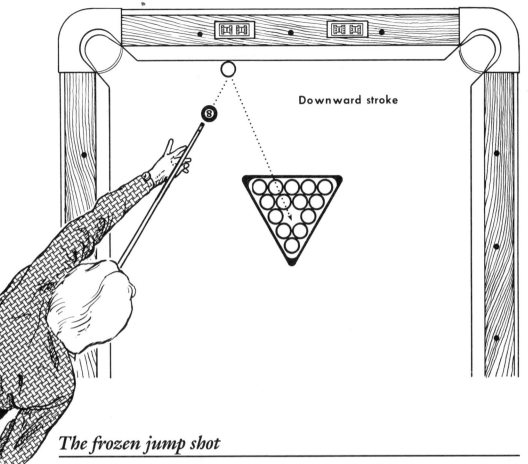

Downward stroke

The frozen jump shot

Professor McCleery was jumping balls into hats this way a hundred years ago. The same technique can be used for racking the last ball, though it's very difficult from the given position. Not too tough if you move the rack of balls a foot closer to the frozen cueball.

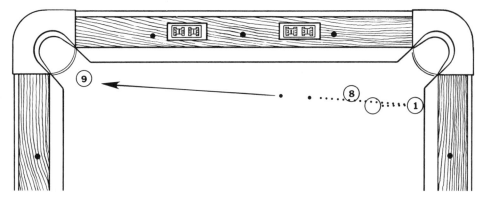

The frozen jump applied

Don't forget that many trick-shot principles can be exploited in games. Old Man McCleery's jump shot in the previous diagram could be used like this in a game of nine-ball.

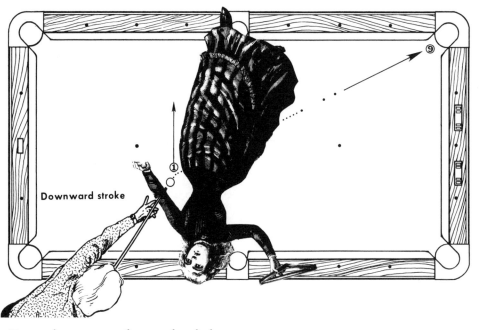

Downward stroke

Jumping over the rack girl

They really did have girls to rack balls in the good old days. If you can't find one for this shot, use your sister. Put her on a table as shown and you can jump a cueball over her to pocket a ball in the corner. I saw the Great Gargani of Argentina make this shot ten years ago at the Palace Billiards in San Francisco using my then nine-year-old son Russell as the obstacle. Russell not only survived, he went on to become a sophomore in college.

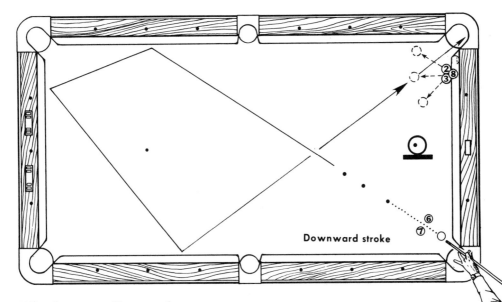

Downward stroke

The jump collapse shot

On page 42 is a shot I called Fred Herrmann's slow collapse. Here's an imaginative use of it. You'll be applauded just for trying. The six and seven are exactly one ball apart. Shooting downward to jump through the gap will shake the pyramid loose at the upper right, if they are set up precariously enough. The eight-ball will roll forward a few inches and stop (middle dashed ball). If the eight gets knocked in by the returning cueball, you are a hero. Does anybody know who thought of this?

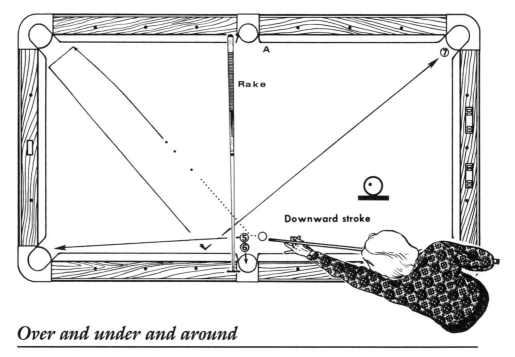

Over and under and around

This shot of Mike Massey's is what led me to think of the one on page 109. Here no props are needed except the rake. With a jump stroke you can send the cueball over rake to start a three-rail journey to the seven. To minimize the length of the jump, put the butt of the rake at A.

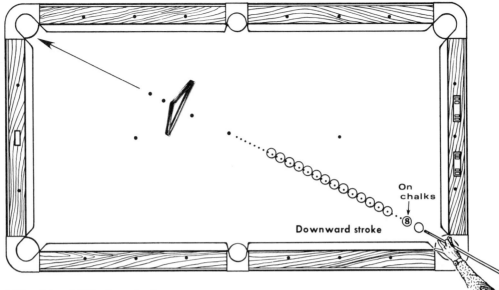

The Evel Knievel shot

Mike Massey also claims this one. The eight is on two pieces of chalk. A downward stroke causes the cueball to rise up under the 8, propelling it over the entire row of balls. It bounces through the upright triangle and into the corner. Allen Hopkins is deadly on this.

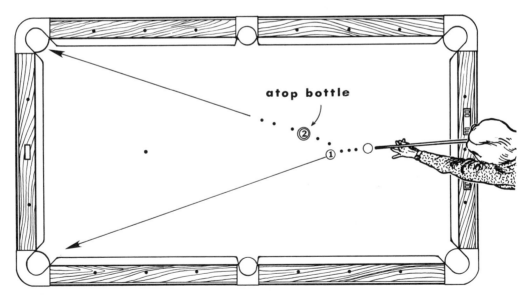

The beer-bottle shot

Knocking a ball off the top of a beer bottle with a jumping cueball, and with the help of another ball used as a ramp, goes back at least fifty years, when the Katsura sisters were doing it in Tokyo. Bill "Weenie Beenie" Staton of Myrtle Beach, South Carolina, has taken the idea and pushed it into the realm of the sensational by *making* the two object balls.

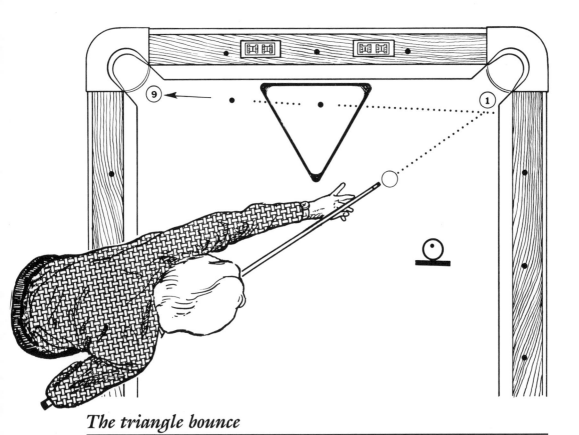

The triangle bounce

San Francisco's venerable Jimmy Lee is a bottomless well of both billiards and pool trickery. He told me he learned this shot in 1910. Elevate your cue, cut in the one, jump into and out of the triangle, and make the nine. A shot for those who like low percentages.

11
Choice Inner Secrets

Clothes make the man.
(Moldenhauer Collection)

I went everywhere, from San Francisco's sleazy South-of-Market saloons to the Library of Congress's marbled vaults; I talked to everybody, from elegant tournament thoroughbreds and obscure theoreticians of the game to the most repellent hustlers and drunks; and I read everything, from crumbling old books to the wretched handwriting of friends from coast to coast. What was I doing? Picking the brains of the living and dead for this book. Pool lore is both endless and growing. Every experienced player seems to have a secret or a subtlety known only to a few. Often beginners and bystanders can offer a nugget picked up from a grandfather or an aunt. (There are plenty of players, though, who apparently intend to tell what they know only to the lids of their coffins.) In this chapter are some of the most closely guarded secrets in the game. There are people who would kill for information like this. Now they won't have to.

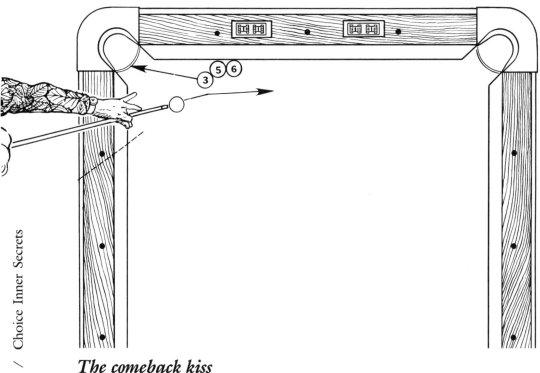

The comeback kiss

Feather the three-ball and it kisses back at an unexpected angle. The dashed line shows how to line up the three-five combination.

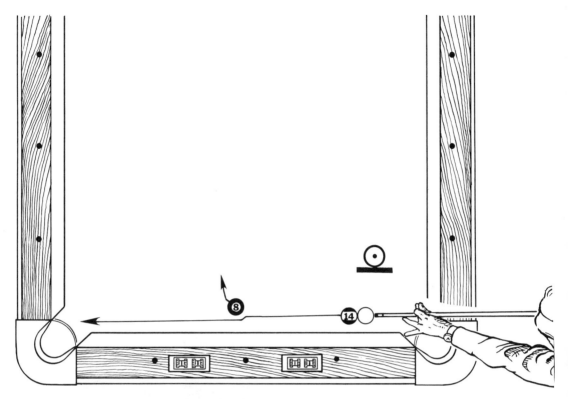

Hippie Jimmy's amazing push

The fourteen and the cueball are frozen and aimed straight at the pocket. The eight-ball is half in the way. Shoot straight through the fourteen and the cueball (sometimes) seems to herd the fourteen into the pocket as if the eight didn't exist. It truly is amazing, as you will see from the expressions on the faces of onlookers. The shot is Jim Reid's, an excellent tournament player who, despite his nickname, looks like a stockbroker.

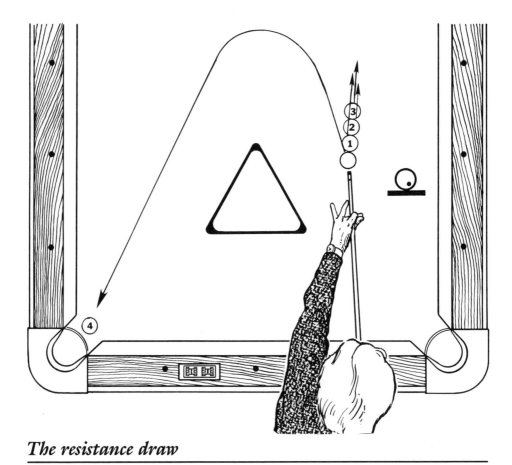

The resistance draw

Provide some resistance for the cueball and a bizarre curve is possible. Don't shoot too hard. I learned this shot watching Willie Mosconi on television. I don't know whence it stems. Right English enables the cuetip to get out of the way.

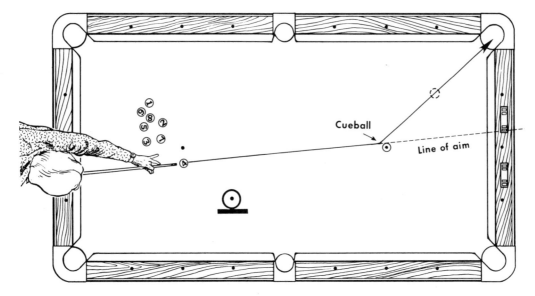

Jewett's repeating in-off

In English billiards, the forerunner of snooker, caroming the cueball off an object ball and into a pocket is called an in-off and is worth points. In the demonstration diagrammed here, the player makes rapid-fire in-offs using a cueball that is repeatedly spotted by an assistant. To be effective, at least two balls should be in motion at all times. Each time the player shoots a ball he grabs another, spots it where the four is in the diagram, and shoots again. The instant the cueball is knocked off the spot, the assistant puts it back. Vital is the spotting of each numbered ball at a point three inches to the right of the head spot (see the four-ball). That enables the shooter to aim for a half-ball hit on the cueball, which causes the moving ball to deflect about forty degrees even if the hit is slightly too full or too thin. (From Bob Jewett.)

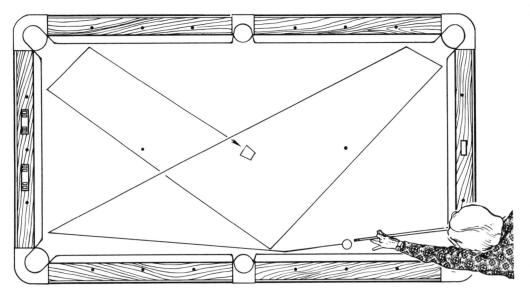

Seven rails to Dixie

Practice this seven-rail bank for a while on a given table and you'll be able to judge rather accurately where the cueball will stop, so accurately that you can make it roll into a Dixie cup. The shot and the name were invented by Myron Zownir. If through secret practice you can learn to make it one time in five, you are ready to accept bets at odds of twenty to one.

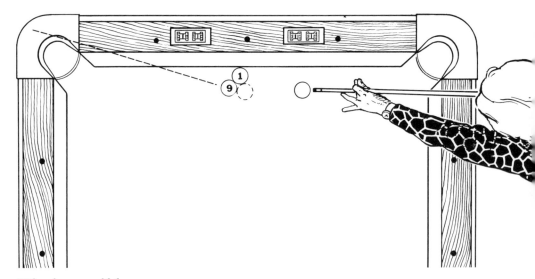

The impossible carom

Freeze the one, the nine, and the cueball together on the rail and aim the cueball-nine combination along the dashed line. Back the cueball off to the position shown. It is obviously impossible to hit the one first and make the nine on a carom. Or is it? The shot can be made by hitting the one full enough to relocate the nine. It's similar to the shot on page 74.

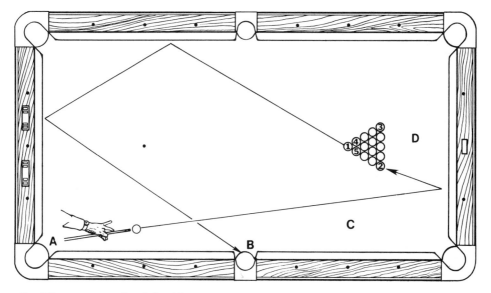

Calling a racked ball

There is no ball that can be called consistently from a full rack of balls. If you insist on calling a ball instead of playing safe, one of the best chances from the above cueball position is banking the two-ball into corner pocket A. Another fairly good one is the one-ball in the side pocket, described in the next diagram. With the cueball at C and the one-ball not on the spot, as it would not be in a straight pool rack, the four can sometimes be banked into side pocket B. From D, the three can be banked into B, though not often. Diagrammed is the two-rail bank of the one, made by banking the cueball into the two from the end rail, which James Coburn does in the 1980 movie *The Baltimore Bullet*. I happened to be on the set the day the shot was filmed. Coburn made it on his first try in the rehearsal. With the cameras running he needed ten.

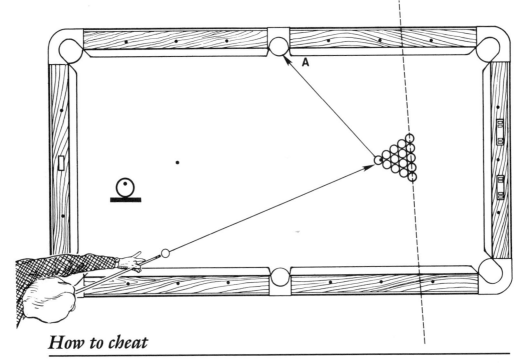

How to cheat

To make the head ball in the side pocket, against which the odds are at least three to one, hit it a hair to the right of center and use follow on the cueball. Sax Dal Porto showed me a way to cheat on the shot, something he would never do himself. Rack the balls slightly *above* the foot spot (note how spot is not in center of head ball) and tilt the rack as indicated by the dashed line. Now your odds are much improved. Your chances of getting out of the joint in one piece, on the other hand, are worse.

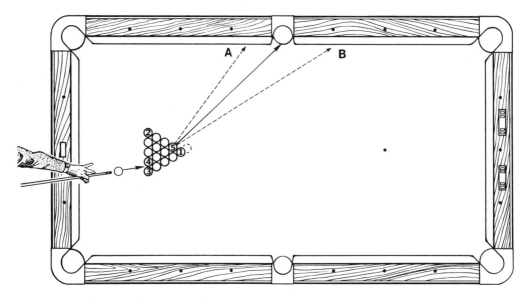

Another full rack shot

When I saw Lou Butera make this in Novato, California, in 1977, I was stunned. He called the five in the side. If the one doesn't get out of the way, the five will hit the rail at A. If the one is gone before the five starts moving, the five will hit at B. Avoid those two extremes and you have a chance. Hit a little of the three before the four. The idea is to relocate the one just enough to guide the five into the side. Everything must be tightly frozen. Lou invented the shot after noticing what happened when a novice tried to play safe.

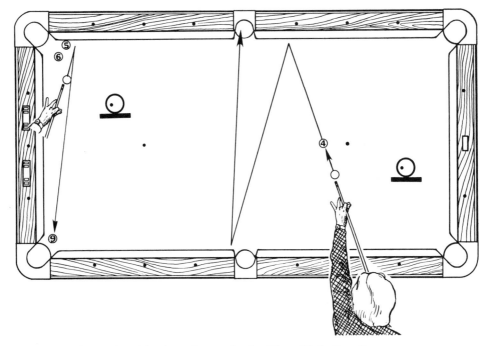

The holdup double bank and the English feather

The shot at the right won't work on some tables. The four is half a diamond from the head spot. Hit it full in the face with maximum left English. If the four hits just beyond the side pocket, there might be enough English left to carry it into the other side pocket. At the left is a problem adapted from a billiard shot shown to me by Abel Calderon, proprietor of King and Queen Billiards in Flushing, New York. It looks impossible, but the nine can be made by hitting the five extremely thin with maximum left English. I mean *extremely* thin. The thing can be done with the cueball even farther to the left.

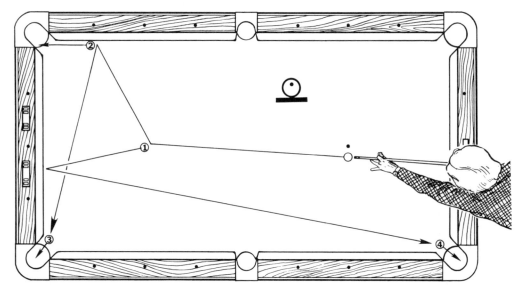

Chris McDonald's best shot

The one-ball is on the spot. Find a position for the cueball so that a half-ball hit will bank the one into the four. When you can do that consistently, note where the cueball hits the first rail. Place the two-ball so that it will cut along the rail. Adjust the speed and the English to make the three as well. The shot is Chris McDonald's.

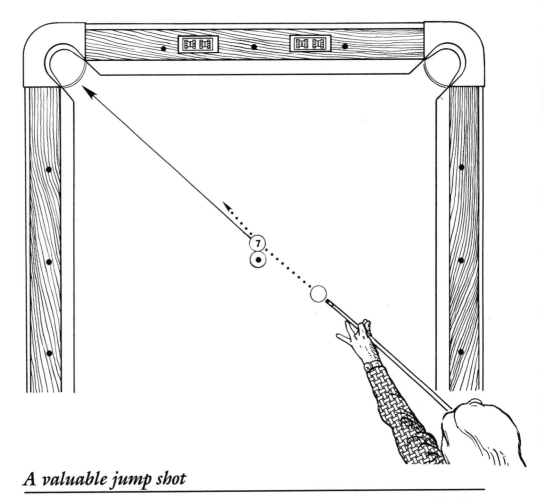

A valuable jump shot

Most players, if they had to hit the seven first in this position, would either bank it or play safe. Mike Massey showed me how to make the seven straight into the corner: shoot down on the cueball and jump over the edge of the interfering ball. The position is not uncommon in ball-in-hand nine-ball.

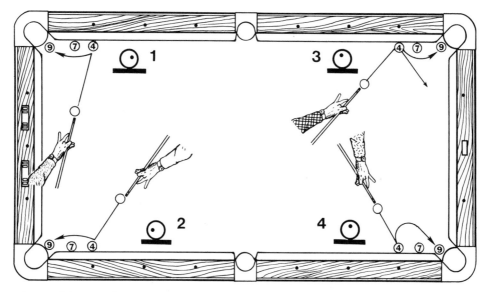

A problem with four solutions

People have been grappling with this situation for 150 years. To make the nine-ball by hitting the four first isn't easy, but it can be done. In shot number one, with the cueball opposite the middle ball, Bill Marshall advises a very soft stroke and high right English. From the position in shot number two, Ray Reardon suggests "side" only. In shot number three, the cueball follows straight through the four, rebounds off the rail enough to clear the seven, then dives forward to make the nine (Michael Phelan, 1858). Shot number four is by far the hardest, in my opinion. Professor McCleery could make it by kissing straight back from the four, then diving forward.

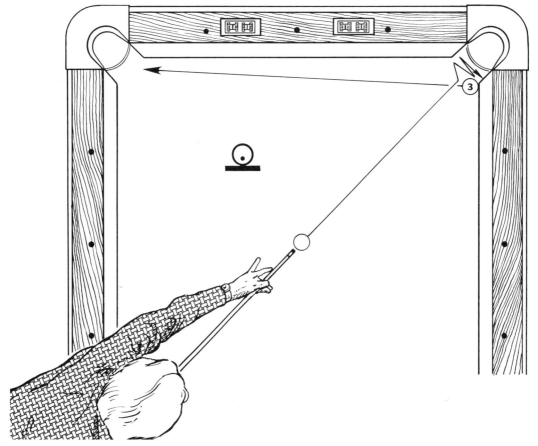

The no-scratch one-pocket bank

In the game of one-pocket, you must make eight balls in your corner pocket before your adversary makes eight in his. It's a game full of clever tactics and strategy. Here is just one example. The three can be banked without scratching. Use draw. Both the kiss and the scratch are avoided by making the cueball rattle back and forth in the jaws. Allen Hopkins is the first player I saw do it.

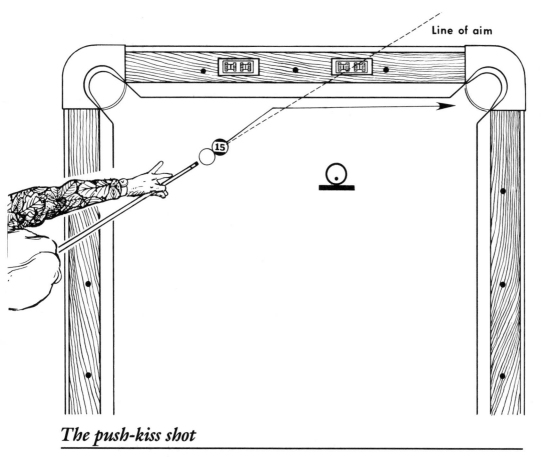

Line of aim

The push-kiss shot

A startling shot when it works. Push straight through the fifteen. The cueball stays with the fifteen and kisses it in when they reach the rail. Tom Kollins of Chicago is my choice as champion of the shot.

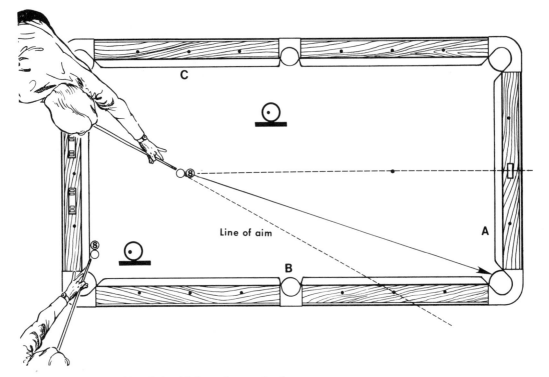

The chalked-ball bank and throw

This diagram and the next are worth the price of the book. Bob Jewett wondered what the effect would be of rubbing chalk on the contact point between two balls, and when he tried it he was richly rewarded. Read carefully. Pick up the cueball and rub a piece of chalk on it to form a spot the size of a cuetip. Freeze it behind a spotted 8-ball as shown, with the chalk spot touching the 8. Believe it or not, the 8 can be thrown into the corner. Aim along the dashed line and use some left English. Sometimes the cueball hits its first rail at A. A more remarkable example is the bank that is set up in the lower left corner of the diagram. Again, the contact point is chalked. Aim at C with left English. The throw and transferred English make it possible to bank the eight into side pocket B. I hate to think of the money that could be won if a player was a big enough skunk to apply the chalk secretly.

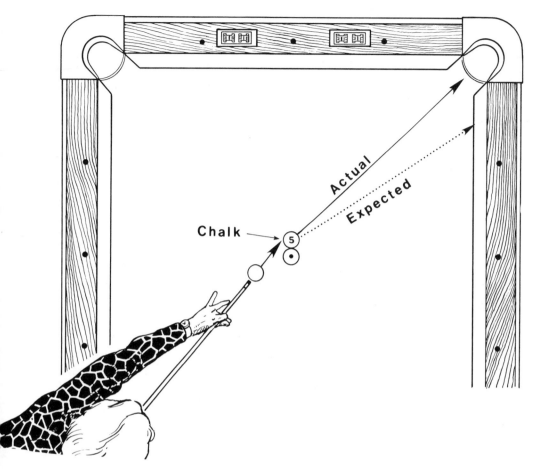

Chalk

Actual

Expected

The chalked-ball cut

Bill Marshall also wondered what would happen if contact points were chalked. Here is one of his discoveries. (He sells diagrams of eleven others.) The five is frozen behind a ball on the spot. Leaving aside the rather reckless jump shot on page 148, can the five be made in the corner without touching the spotted ball? It can if there is chalk on the side of the five at the right place. Cut the five slightly with a little right English. Instead of traveling along the dotted line as it should, it will go straight ahead into the pocket, provided you have some skill and have invested some practice time.

Chalked-ball shots demonstrate vividly the importance of playing with clean balls. The dirtier they are, the more they will stick together and "throw." Slovenly proprietors please note.

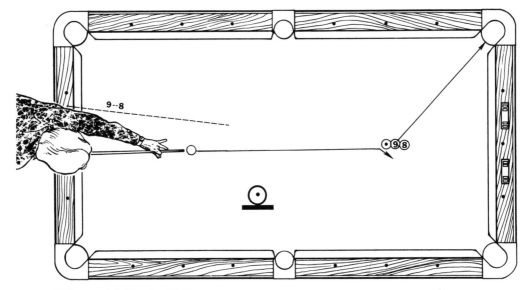

The middle-ball force

From this position it is possible to make the middle ball in the corner. The trick lies in lining up the rear ball about an eighth of inch off center. I get the best results by hitting the spot ball not quite full, as indicated by the arrow. Hard stroke. A choice inner secret if ever there was one, which my readers, I have no doubt, will use only in an ethical manner. (From Anonymous, 1918.)

12
Personal Favorites

On certain shots it is important to cut down the length of the backswing.
(Moldenhauer Collection)

In this chapter are seventeen shots of varying types. Some are easy, some are hard. Some are technical, some are showy. They have only one thing in common; for one reason or another, they are personal favorites of mine.

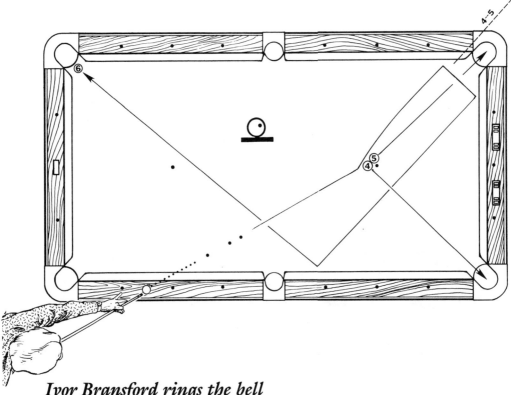

Ivor Bransford rings the bell

Here's a good one from Ivor Bransford. It's flashy, easy to set up, and well within the reach of the highly gifted. If the cueball won't stay on the rail, Ivor suggests leaning it against a piece of chalk.

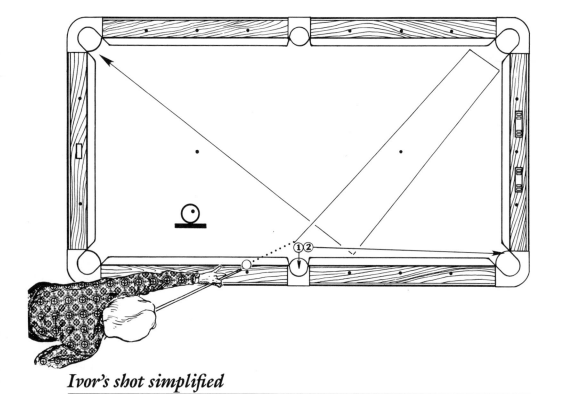

Ivor's shot simplified

If the previous shot is too tough, try this version. It's a cinch and almost as flashy.

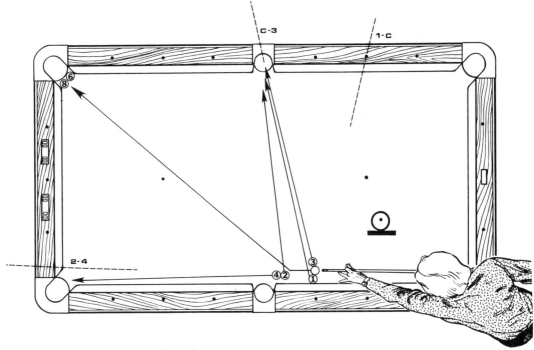

The Denver sandwich

Note how the cueball is between two object balls on the rail one diamond from the side and note how they are aimed. A stroke parallel to the rail sends both object balls across the table and into the side. I call the formation the Denver Sandwich after Bob Nicholl of that Colorado city, who invented it. One way he makes use of the idea is shown. The one, two, and three rushing one after the other into the side is a pleasing effect. Good luck on making both the eight and the six.

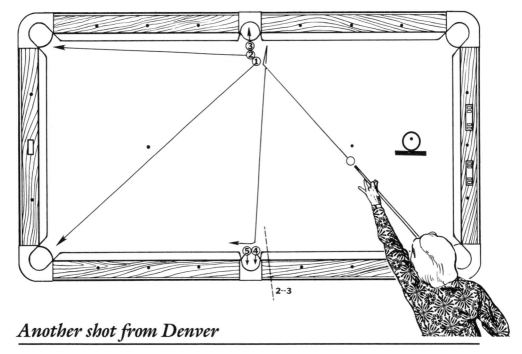

Another shot from Denver

This has to be struck fairly hard to make sure the one-ball reaches its destination. Note how the two and three line up (dashed line). (Nicholl.)

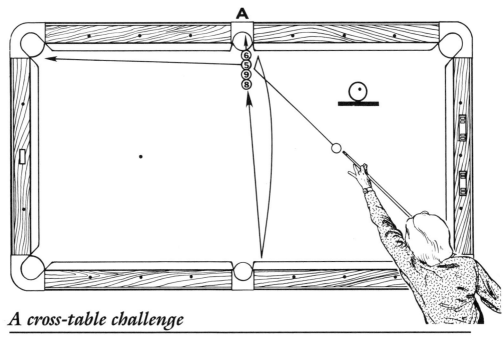

A cross-table challenge

Set the balls up like this and see if anybody can figure out a way to make the nine-ball in side pocket A. My solution is to go twice across off the five. By the time the cueball hits the eight, the five and six are long gone. Omit the eight and more precision is needed.

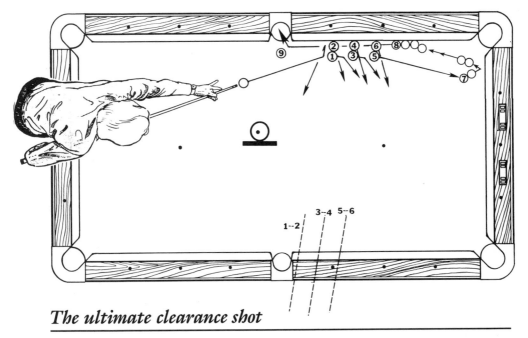

The ultimate clearance shot

This goes back many years, exactly how many I don't know. (Maybe you do.) After the balls are in position, announce that the eight will go in the side. "Huh?" everybody will say, or words to that effect. This would be in the chapter on classic shots if it was easier to set up.

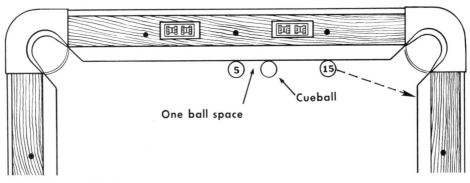

Cueball

One ball space

Jewett's rail draw trap

I've nailed at least ten of the nation's top players with this challenge, invented by Bob Jewett. Freeze three balls on the rail in the indicated positions. The challenge is to pocket the fifteen and draw back to merely touch the five. Even the loftiest champions think they can do it; in fact, it is very nearly impossible. After they find they can't make it, they don't know why. The reason for the difficulty is that part of the cueball is *under* the nose of the rail; that is, the nose of the rail slightly overlaps the edge of the ball. The position of the five forces a steep cue angle if draw is to be put on the cueball. Since a downward stroke forces the cueball to jump, it squirts away from under the rail, which often makes the fifteen travel along the dashed line instead of into the pocket. Don't pass this by; it's one of the gems of the book.

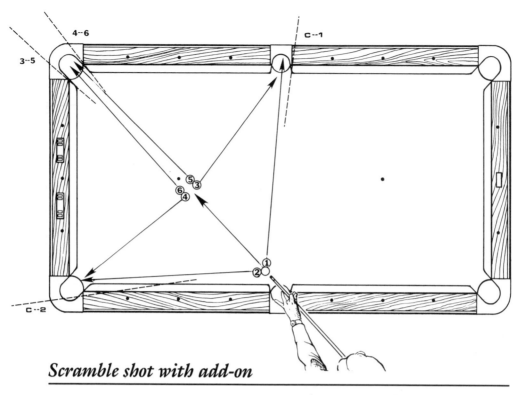

Scramble shot with add-on

You could hardly ask for a better show shot than what Jimmy Caras calls scramble. The above diagram clarifies the position. Adding the one and two makes it harder but elevates it into the showstopping category.

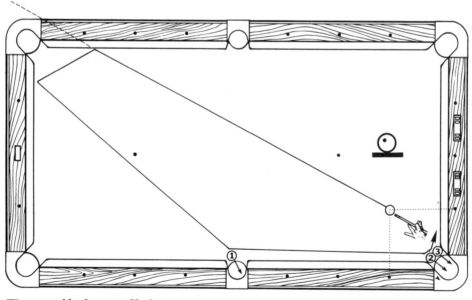

Two-rail show-off shot

Not as hard as it looks if you have a chance to practice it a few times to find the exact aiming point. According to Tommy Thomsen, Willie Mosconi made it in a 1964 exhibition in Tucson, Arizona, just after running 138 and out in straight pool.

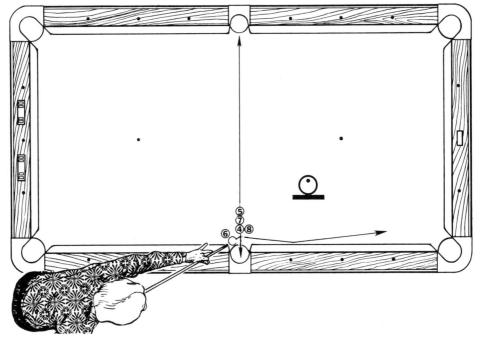

Byrne's side-pocket surprise

I was trying to invent a shot in which a combination would send a ball across the table and back into the same combination balls, pocketing something else, but the balls wouldn't stay put no matter how I reinforced them with other balls. The first ball contacted by the cueball sometimes backed up in a way I would never have predicted, which led to the invention of the shot diagrammed above. How many players would guess that the four-ball can be made in the near side pocket? Damned few. Shoot hard across the face of the four with high follow. Enough English gets transferred to draw the four into the side. Very surprising. To me, anyway.

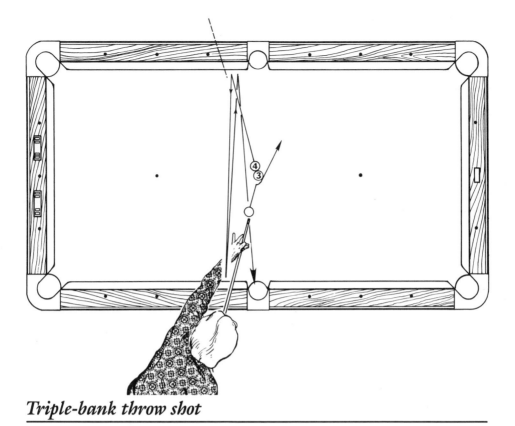

Triple-bank throw shot

I'm deeply in love with this shot of Bill Marshall's. The dashed line indicates how the three-four are aimed. The three is on the center of the table. Hitting the three full not only throws the four to the right but imparts some right English. The result is that the four triple banks in the side with good regularity. He suggests hitting the cueball low; high right seems to work best for me.

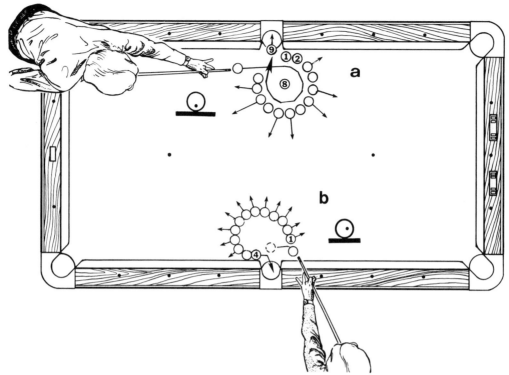

The inner circle and the frozen ring

Two of my inventions. Shot A bears a resemblance to ring around the rosy (Caras, page 32). With draw, the cueball can be made to trace a complete circle to pocket the nine. The one must be feathered to make sure it doesn't bank across to spoil things. The way the balls are arranged in the diagram, it would be advisable to miss the one and hit the two first. My thanks to Myron Zownir for suggesting placing the eight-ball in the middle, which adds interest. In Shot B, the idea is to hit the one-ball, then make the four on a carom. All the balls must be frozen or the four won't pop out. The right English is merely to help keep the cue from fouling the cueball. In setting up the ring of balls, start with the one a ball and a half from the rail.

Easy-action four-ball shot

An ideal exhibition shot: easy to arrange, easy to make, and interesting to watch. Use plenty of follow. (Shown to me by Mike Sigel.)

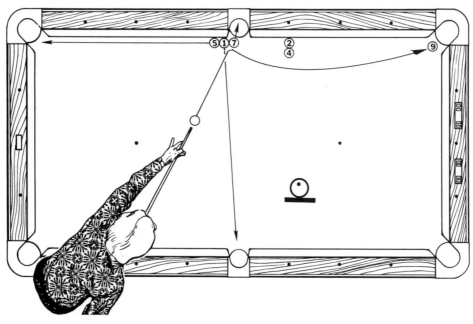

Easy action with bank

Here the cueball diverges from the rail, then dives forward. Omit the obstacle balls till you get the hang of it. Hit the one quite thin. For more diving action, start with the cueball a couple of inches to the right. (Anonymous.)

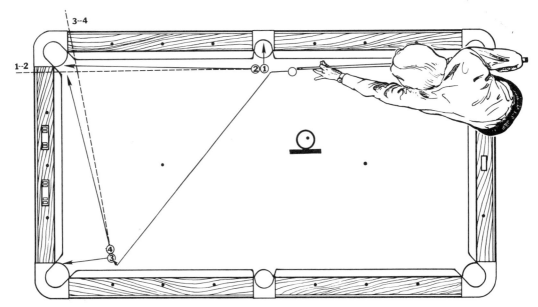

Paul Lucchesi, Sr.'s, shot

A good player with practice should be able to make all four balls at least one time in three. Named after Paul Lucchesi, Sr., because without him I wouldn't have had access to Anonymous, from which the idea is taken.

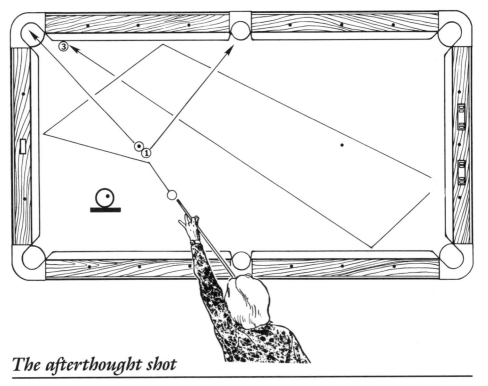

The afterthought shot

The three-ball is pocketed long after the other two, almost as an afterthought. Don't hit the one-ball too full or the cueball will lose too much speed. (Anonymous.)

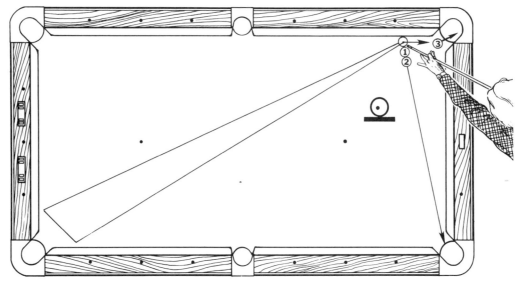

Thread the needle

I enjoy shooting this because onlookers don't think you have a chance in the world. The odds against aren't quite that high. The object is to bank the frozen cueball around the table so that it goes through a hole that is smaller than a ball to make the three. The two goes for good measure. Aim, speed, and English must be blended perfectly. (Anonymous.)

13

The Great and the Near Great

The shorter the shot the easier it is, generally speaking.
(*Illustrated Police News,* 1888)

Whether a shot should be called great, excellent, or merely good depends ultimately on the prejudice of the labeler, i.e., me. There are, of course, objective criteria as well. Can it be made a high enough percentage of the time to keep the audience from slipping into a coma? Is it so hard on the equipment that the proprietor has to be put under sedation? I like the following eighteen shots, but I frankly don't know if they should be called great or good. I can't make some of them consistently, but the flaw may lie with me and not the shots.

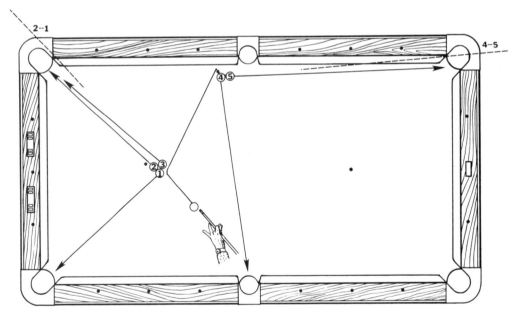

Central cluster add-on

Once you can make the three balls in the central cluster consistently, note where the cueball hits the first rail and add the four and five. (Nicholl.)

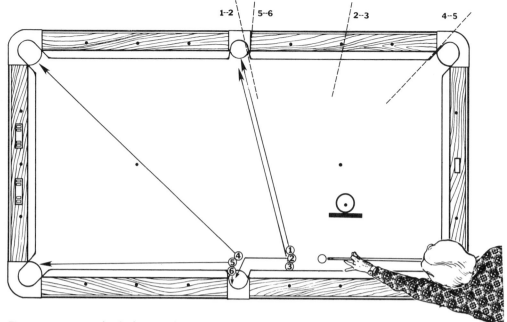

Denver sandwich variation

One page 158, the sandwich filler was the cueball; here it's the 2. Bob Nicholl suggests practicing first with just the one, two, and three until you can make the two go down the table parallel to the rail. Then add the four, five, and six. If you decide the four, five, and six should not be frozen, the indicated combination lines will have to be adjusted.

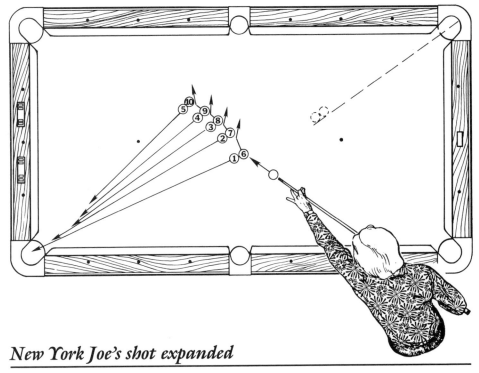

New York Joe's shot expanded

New York Joe Bachelor spent the last part of his life in San Francisco conferring nightly with Bud Harris and Jimmy Lee. Before moving west he showed a shot involving three pairs of balls to Myron Zownir, who later expanded it to five pairs. In the diagram, a full, hard hit on the six-ball is supposed to pocket the one, two, three, four, and five. The space between the pairs should be about a ball. Position the pairs so that the outside balls strike the next in line about half full. At the right are dashed lines showing a method of lining up the pairs quickly with a cue, an idea of Norm Smith's.

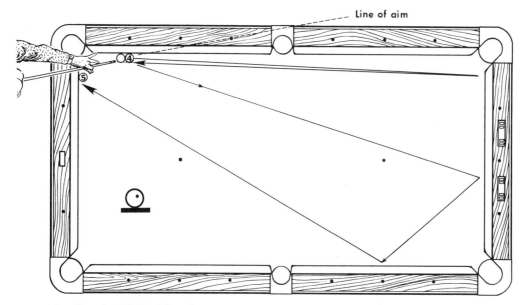

A Cueball Kelly shot

The venerable Cueball Kelly is famous for this one. The four-ball banks in the corner and the cueball goes around the table to cut in the five.

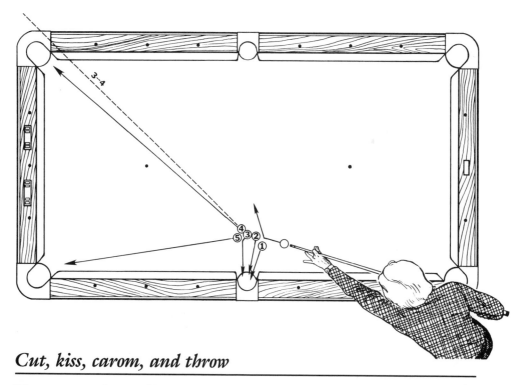

Cut, kiss, carom, and throw

The one cuts, the two kisses, the three caroms, and the four throws. If you fuss with this long enough, you can make the five, too. Note the gap between the three and five. The cut on the one should be such that it beats the two to the pocket. (Original.)

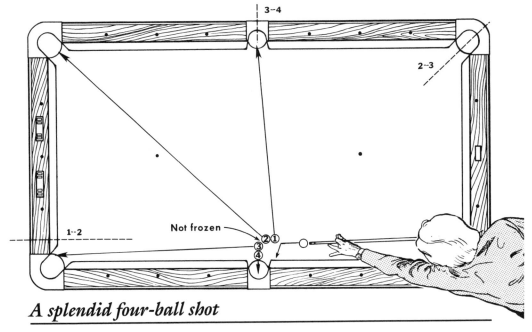

A splendid four-ball shot

Once you learn exactly how to position the two in relation to the three, you have a splendid shot to add to your repertoire. Only when you can make it three times in four should you think about making the cueball do additional work. (From Anonymous.) The gap is recommended by Paul Gerni.

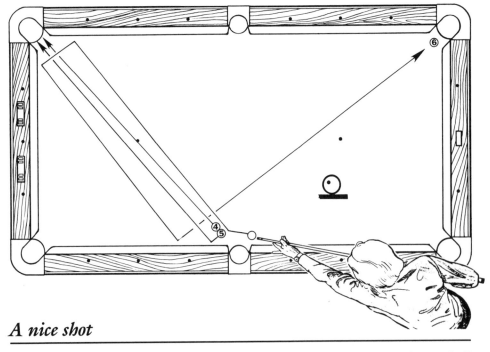

A nice shot

The distance between the rail and the five is one ball. Note that the cueball beats the object balls to the corner. (Anonymous.)

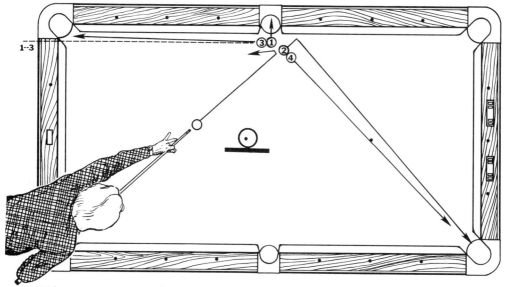

The purse snatcher

The two goes in before the four. Because the two hits the four so thinly, you don't have to allow for throw when aligning the two-four combination. Paul Gerni calls the shot the purse snatcher because of a story that goes along with it. One thing led to another and he forgot to tell me the story.

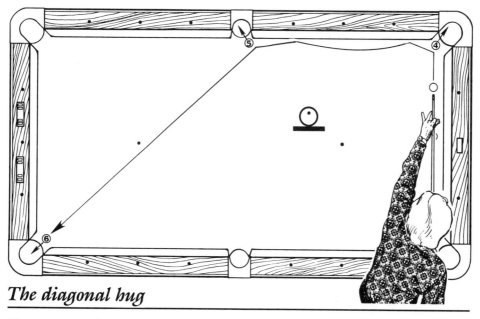

The diagonal hug

If you can pocket the four and keep the cueball hugging the rail with follow until it makes the five, you have a good chance of crossing the table diagonally to make the six. (Shown to Gerni by Ambrose.) Those who wish to combine an exhibition of trick shots with a lecture on etymology will want to know that the word "hugging" in the sense used here goes back at least to 1858. (See Phelan, page 123.)

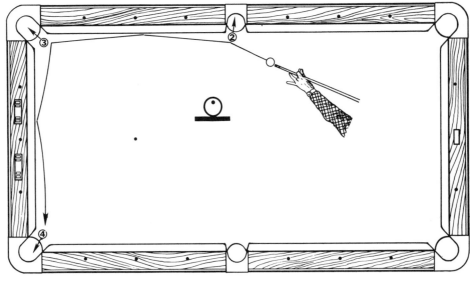

Another hug shot

The crowd will love it if you get good hugging action after making the three.

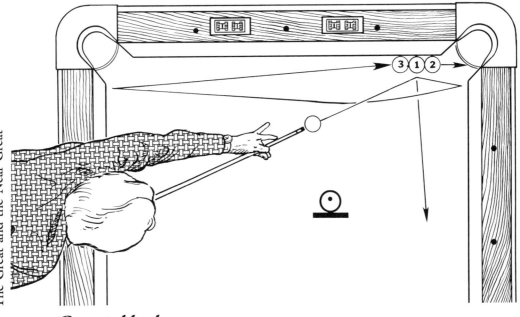

Cross-table clearance

Hit the one, make the two, bank the one, and cross the table twice to make the three. The cueball comes off the first rail before the one has moved enough to kiss it. A little high is needed to bend the cueball path toward the three as it crosses the table. Tough shot. (Nicholl.)

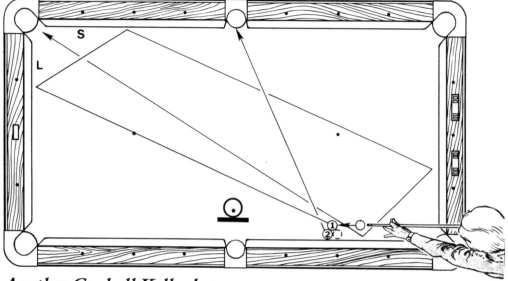

Another Cueball Kelly shot

The two-ball banks and the one goes four rails into the corner. The dashed circle shows where to put the cueball when aligning the one and two. A fairly hard stroke is needed. If the one reaches the upper left area short (S), put right English on the cueball next time. If it goes long (L), use left.

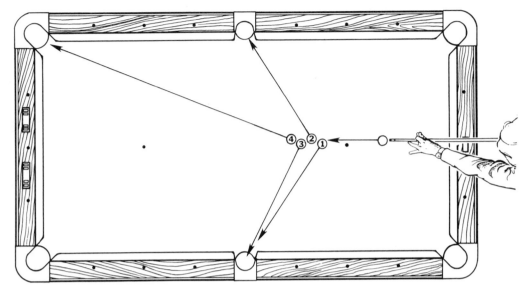

Hallucination modified

I was awakened suddenly one night by a vision of a sinuous row of balls dividing the middle of the table and a cueball approaching from the right at a high rate of speed. Pow! Seven flew into one side pocket, seven into the other, and one into the corner. "Good God," I cried, sitting upright and throwing the covers aside, "would that work?" Fortunately, I was alone at the time. In dawn's cold light I could see that six or seven balls total was probably all that could be hoped for. Later that same day in Novato, California, after an hour of frustrating work on Lee Simon's finest table, my dreams of discovering something truly sensational were in ashes at my feet. Four balls seemed to be the limit, and even then the shot was chancy. Bob Jewett took over the field research at that point while I moved on to the next chapter. His final report showed that a tiny gap should be left between each pair of balls and that the first ball should be struck so it beats the third ball to the pocket. A lot of speed is needed to transmit sufficient impetus to the four. Can anyone out there carry the idea further?

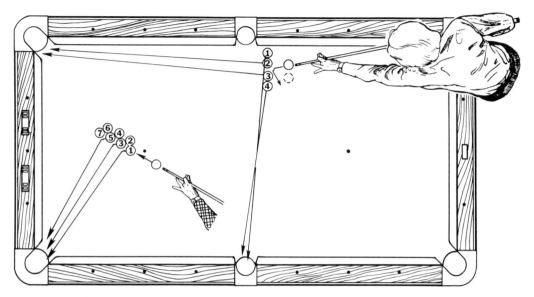

Two unsolved problems

Jess Meshanic sent me a clipping from the December 20, 1935, *New York Evening Journal*. It was an article on the great Irwin Rudolph. A photo of the four-time world champion showed him in the midst of a confusing trick shot. Superimposed arrows suggested that the camera had caught three balls in the act of emerging from a pack on their way to the corner pocket. An accompanying diagram, intended to make the position clear, was an impenetrable muddle. Not until 1981 was the code deciphered, and then only partially, by Bob Jewett. In the seven-ball cluster at the left, there are gaps between the one, three, five, and seven. Struck as shown, the two guides the one into the three, the four guides the three into the five, and the six guides the five into the seven so that the one, three, and five go into the corner. That's the guts of the Irwin shot. Can anybody figure out how to make it a dependable idea?

The four-ball arrangement at the top of the diagram is an idea of mine that looks as though it should work. The way the one follows the four into the bottom side looks good . . . when the one doesn't overtake the four and kiss it out. The three either goes directly into the corner or it banks in the corner, depending on the hit and the English on the cueball, or it goes nowhere. My instincts tell me that the right positioning and hit can be found, but I haven't found them yet. Making all four is still no more than a one-in-seven proposition, which isn't good enough. Bill Marshall reports good results by approaching the cluster from the position of the dashed ball.

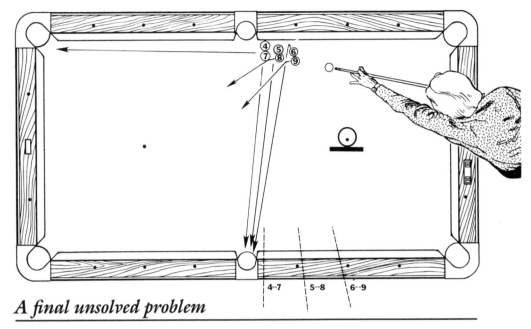

A final unsolved problem

From a notebook full of unsolved problems, I present one more. The solution seems tantalizingly near. Because laymen love to see bank shots, I tried to find a way to bank three or four at once. In the diagram, the four, five, and six are supposed to bank in the side. They will sometimes. The trick is to find a method of setting them up so they'll do it consistently. Then maybe a fourth pair could be added.

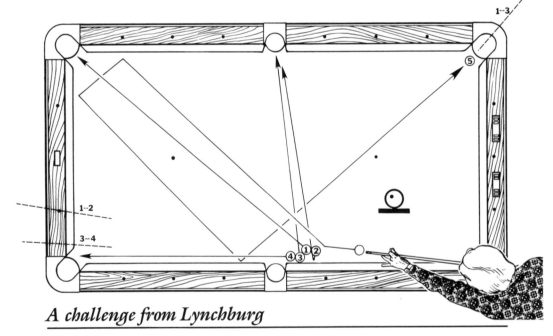

A challenge from Lynchburg

A Bill Marshall original. If you learn to make the five balls in sequence, tear this page out and paste into the chapter on showstoppers.

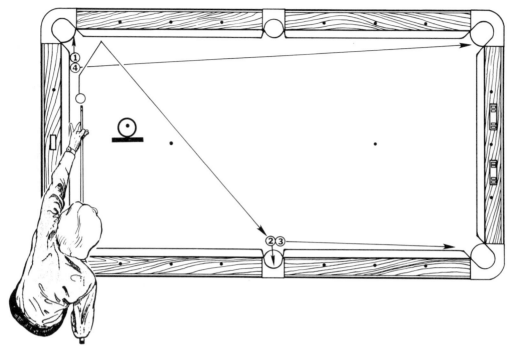

A four-ball shot

First find the hit that makes the four-ball, then adjust the English so that the cueball hits the two-ball. (Anonymous.)

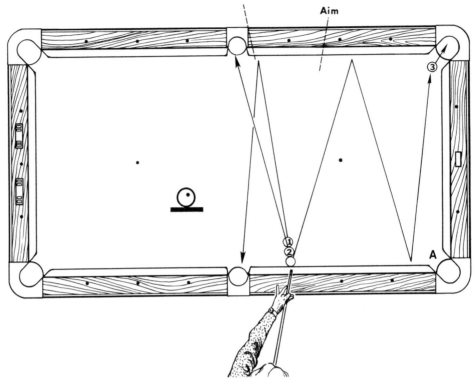

The multiple criss-cross

The book by Anonymous is full of good stuff, but the murky diagrams omit such details as exactly where to put the balls. It's like trying to read one of those musical scores by J. S. Bach that doesn't give the tempo, the phrasing, or even the instruments. In the shot above, the lead ball is supposed to bank in the side, the middle ball to go directly into the opposite side, and the cueball to bank once or twice to make a ball in the corner. I spent a lot of time (and what thanks do I get?) coming up with the aiming line, the combination line, and the English recommended in the diagram. Maybe you can find improvements.

14
Stroke Shots

Try not to let your opponent get under your skin.
(Moldenhauer Collection)

We all like to watch the exploits of Walter Payton, Julius Irving, and Nadia Comenici, which doesn't mean we think we can do what they do. That's the spirit of this chapter. Here are feats far beyond the reach of the average player. Don't even look at the diagrams unless you are emotionally prepared to accept that you will never be able to make at least ten of the next eighteen shots. Never. Ever. Even if you have a practice table you are willing to slash to pieces. For reasons I don't pretend to understand, God has endowed some people with the ability to do more with a cueball than the rest of us. Believe me, you'll save yourself a lot of heartache and damage claims if you'll treat this chapter as entertainment and not as instruction. Think of it as a visit to a planet inhabited by giants who are both gifted and maniacal. I fervently hope that the next few pages don't touch off a wave of miniature demolition derbies in the pool halls and saloons of this great land.

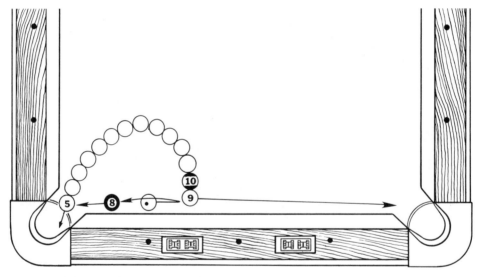

The Bill Hughes massé shot

Maybe the introduction to this chapter was tainted by rhetorical excess. Many massé shots aren't quite as hard as they look and can be made by average players with proper coaching and a decent cue. If you have both, try this unusual shot invented by Bill Hughes of Morgan Hill, California. Arrange the semicircle of frozen balls so that the nine is about half a ball space from the rail. Massé the cueball into the nine with enough speed to pocket the nine as well as the five. The cueball, if all goes well, will back up and pocket the eight. It's easier if the eight is closer to the five.

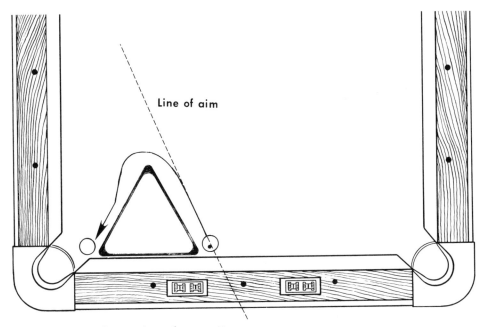

The triangle-assisted massé

Massé around a triangle to make a ball hanging on the lip. If the cueball breaks too soon, the triangle guides it in the right direction.

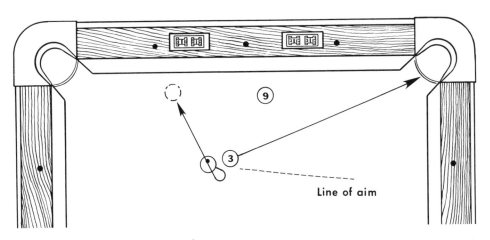

An exquisite position shot

The action here is so beautiful it will give you goose bumps. The problem is to make the three and gain position on the nine. Approached normally, the cueball will not end up very favorably because the required line of aim to cut the three will send it far from the nine. A massé shot, with the cue almost vertical, can bring the cueball back along the path diagrammed, which would be especially profitable in a game of one-pocket. The cueball must be quite close to the three or the shot becomes too difficult. With just a few exceptions, executing this shot perfectly gives me more pleasure than anything else in life.

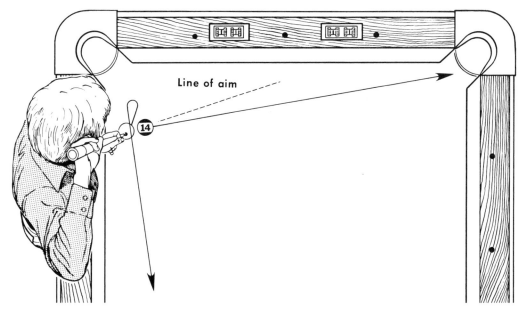

Length-of-the-table position massé

Similar to the previous shot. The fourteen is straight in. How can you get the cueball to the other end of the table and still make the fourteen? With a massé shot. The angled line of aim is needed because the cueball spin will throw the fourteen. Cuemaker Bob Meucci has the shot down cold.

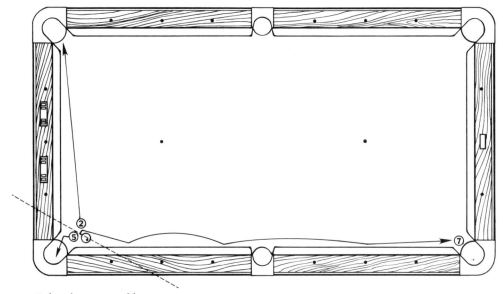

The long-rail massé

One of Willie Mosconi's specialties. He gets tremendous action on the ball. A sharp massé stroke will sink the five and the two and keep the cueball on the rail, accelerating as it goes, to sink the seven.

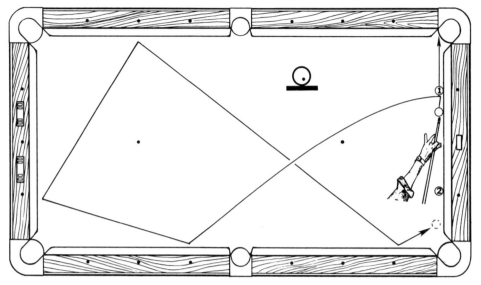

The one-pocket power draw

This is one of those shots you may never live to make. It takes a pile-driver stroke. The challenge is to make the one-ball and get position to make the two *in the same pocket*. The seemingly impossible solution is to shoot slightly into the rail with extreme low right and hit it a ton. Lots of luck. Notice that I have my sleeve rolled up.

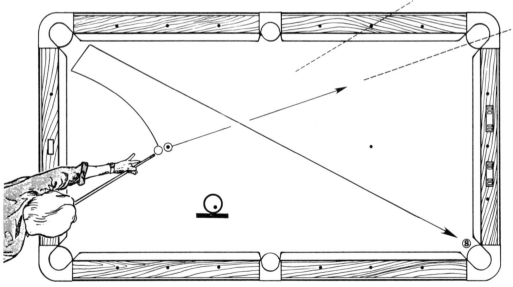

Two-rail power draw

Another shot I have to roll up my sleeve for. The cueball and the spotted ball are lined up for the corner pocket. Aim at the second diamond from the corner with low right and try to draw the cueball two rails into the eight. Just hitting three rails is deserving of applause. The hit on shots like this is not nearly as important as the stroke, so concentrate on delivering the cue straight through the cueball.

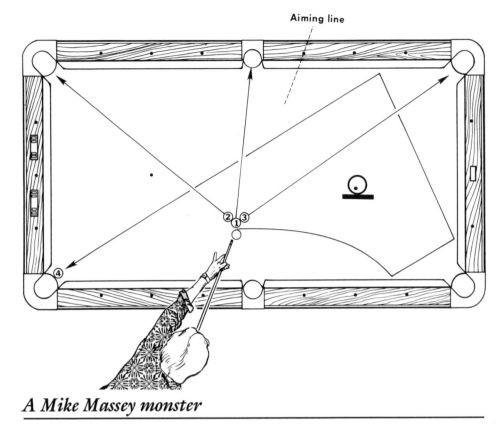

Aiming line

A Mike Massey monster

When Mike Massey makes shots like this, the rest of us look like sissies.

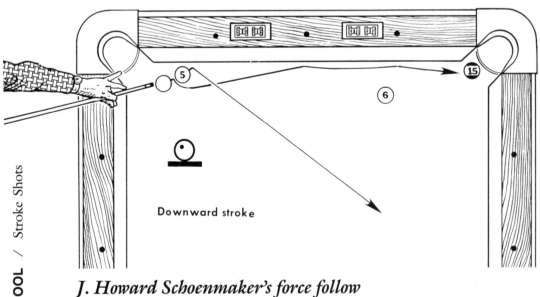

Downward stroke

J. Howard Schoenmaker's force follow

J. Howard Schoenmaker, who won the national amateur pool title nine times between 1913 and 1935, was photographed shooting this and other shots for the May 4, 1935, edition of *Collier's* magazine. (Thank you, Jess Meshanic.) The six is there to make it seem impossible.

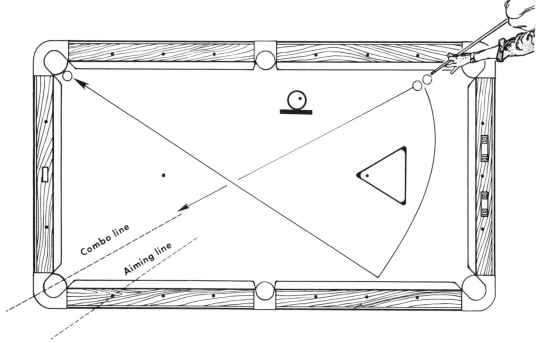

A force-follow bank shot

Not for children. Elevate the cue about twenty degrees from the horizontal, shoot hard, and drive the tip straight through the cueball along the indicated line of aim. We have Bob Jewett to blame for this shot as well as the next one.

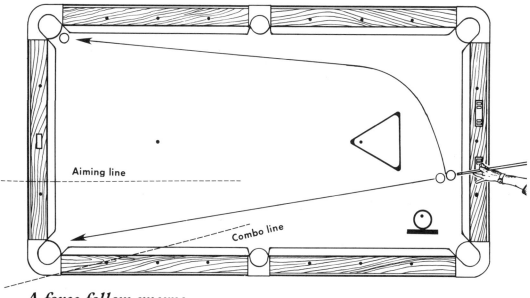

A force-follow swerve

Don't bet on it.

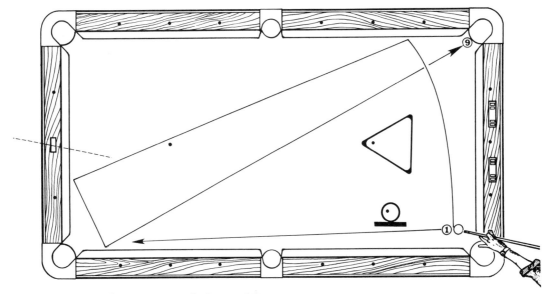

Force follow around the table

Trying to make the previous shot made me think of this one. When setting it up, remember to allow for throw on the one-ball. Aim along the dashed line. Shoot hard. Elevate.

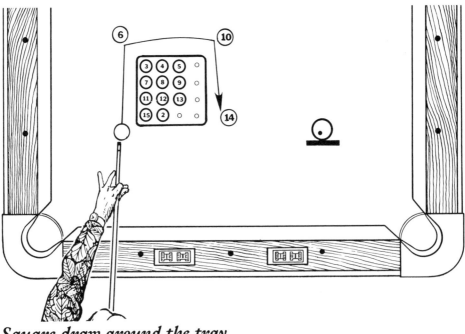

Square draw around the tray

Noriko Katsura, the best female cueperson in the world today, showed this shot on her last visit from Tokyo. All you have to do is use draw to make the cueball hit three object balls. The tray is not strictly necessary, but it helps guide the cueball when the hit isn't perfect.

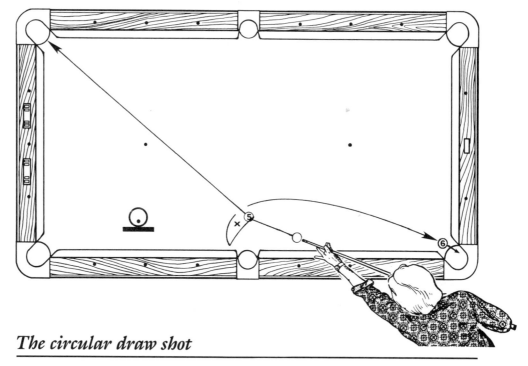

The circular draw shot

Mike Massey's cue comes forward like a piston, the five rockets into the corner, and the cueball follows the goofy path in the diagram to make the six. I've quit trying the shot and am learning to accept life on a lower plateau. A hundred years ago, Professor McCleery called this the circular draw shot. In his version, the cueball bent around a second ball spotted at point X.

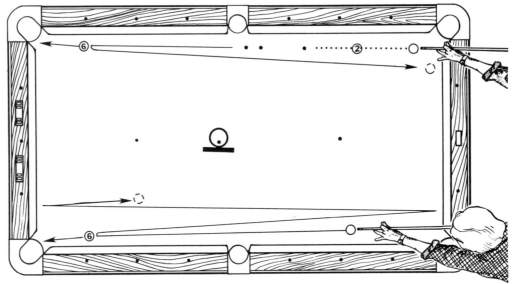

Two King Kong draw shots

I hesitated including this diagram for fear that stores would stock this book in the science-fiction department. At the bottom of the diagram, the player is pocketing the six and drawing the cueball two table lengths. At the top, the cueball jumps *over* the two, pockets the six, and draws back the length of the table. I saw Mike Massey perform both of these stunts in 1981 at the Caesar's Tahoe Billiard Classic on George Middleditch's exhibition table. He was successful on the first try with each shot. It was enough to make a person sick.

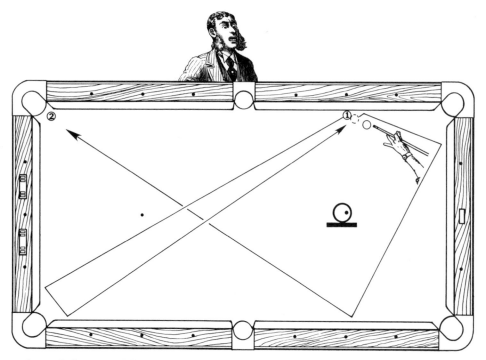

The ultimate kiss-around

One of the most amazing shots in the repertoire. The inventor is unknown, but three-cushion players were shooting versions of it ninety years ago. Eddie Robin, twice national three-cushion king, showed it to me in 1979 at the Denver Athletic Club. He made it on the first try. Life is hard. All you have to do is hit the one and leave the cueball spinning in place so that when the one returns it will knock the cueball three rails into the two. A mere bagatelle. I think your money would be safe giving ten-to-one odds to anybody.

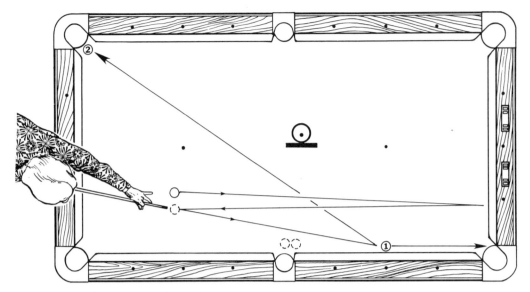

Snooks Perlstein's shot

Snooks Perlstein of Atlantic City, New Jersey, tried to make this shot off and on for sixty years, finally succeeding in the summer of 1981. Now he's trying to make it again. Having a goal in life is what keeps him looking so young. Bank the cueball the length of the table; when it returns, hit it again, pocketing the one-ball and drawing back diagonally to pocket the two-ball. Don't use too much draw on the second hit or the moving cueball will climb over your tip. The action usually sought on double stroke shots can be seen in Caras, page 52.

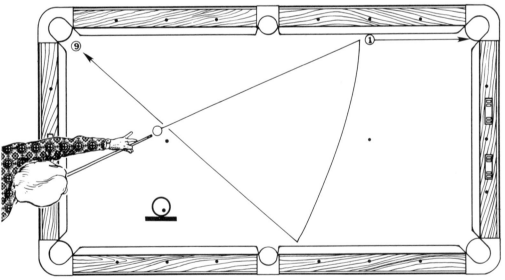

Tom Smith's reverse draw

If you are good enough to make this shot, you are probably well on your way toward getting expelled from school, fired from your job, and divorced by your spouse. Tom Smith of Kearny, New Jersey, the inventor, who as far as I know is none of the above, recommends a complete follow-through and a loose wrist.

15
Hot Lips and Magic Fingers

In tavern league matches, disagreements over rules should be resolved by team captains, if necessary by a flip of a coin.
(Moldenhauer Collection)

If you aren't so hot with a cue, you might try spinning the cueball onto the table with a snap of the fingers or blowing it out of your mouth. Finger billiards, a form of juggling, has a long history. It was invented, according to John A. Thatcher's *Championship Billiards Old and New* (1898) by Jake "The Wizard" Schaefer, who could "spin the wee spheres" to great effect. The best, though, Thatcher assures us, was H. T. Perry of Cincinnati, Ohio, who "executes with any size ball up to two and seven-sixteenths inches and at cushion caroms picks up his ball wherever he finds it." The best finger billiardists I know about today are eighty-four-year-old Cueball Kelly of New York, Mike Massey of Chattanooga, and Juan Navarra of Buenos Aires. Perhaps publication of the following chapter will bring more practitioners out of the closet. It may be, in fact, that a renaissance of finger billiards is about to flower around us, thanks to the coin-operated bar pool table. On a bar table, you see, you can fool around with the cueball free of charge.

Schuster explained in a letter to Ripley that the tenth ball was out of sight in the palm of his hand, which must have been gargantuan.

Ripley's—**Believe It or Not!**

SAM SICHERMAN
New York City

PLAYS POCKET BILLIARDS
WITH HIS MOUTH —
FREQUENTLY MAKING
RUNS OF **15** AND

HE PUTS THE BALL IN HIS MOUTH
AND **BLOWS** IT OUT AGAINST THE OBJECT
BALL

© RIPLEY INTERNATIONAL LIMITED 1938

Blow-pool—blowing a ball onto the table from the mouth—is an even more obscure specialty. I can't do it because I can't get a ball into my mouth, not even a snooker ball. I would try stretching exercises if I didn't suspect that in some respects my mouth is already too big. Steve Simpson of Tennessee is perhaps the best known blow-pool artist. My sources assure me that he can expel a pool ball with such explosive force that it will hit seven rails. For more see the July 1972 issue of the *National Billiard News*.

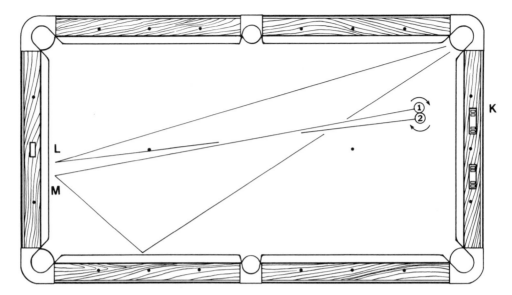

The pumpkin-seed squirt

Stand at K and lay your hand over the one and two, squeezing them together with the thumb and middle finger. Squeeze hard enough and they will begin to leave your hand, rotating against each other like cogwheels in the direction of the small arrows. As this happens throw them toward the opposite rail with a sweeping motion, making sure the one-ball gets ahead of the two. Done right the one will hit at M and bank two rails into the corner and the two will hit L and bank one rail. There's a knack to it, if I may be permitted an understatement. (Cueball Kelly.)

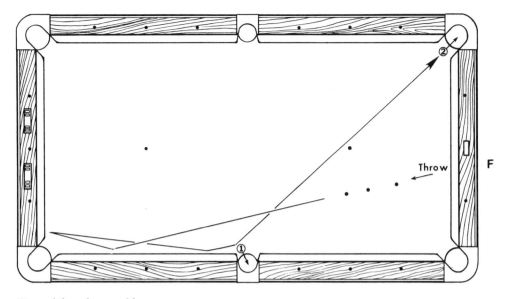

Double the rail

Stand at F. With a finger-snapping motion of the right hand, throw the cueball as shown, with clockwise spin. The cueball is supposed to double the rail and make both the one and the two. Cueball Kelly asks five tries.

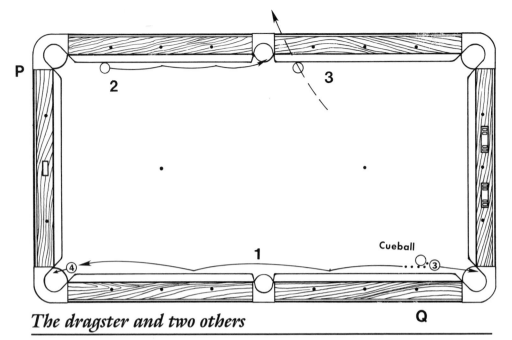

The dragster and two others

Holding the cueball about six inches above the table (shot one), Mike Massey, standing at Q, tosses the cueball into the three. The spin he induces by snapping his fingers (thumb on top snaps forward, middle finger underneath snaps back) causes the cueball to spurt along the rail to make the four. Because of the way it seems to shift gears while accelerating, he has dubbed it the dragster. Standing at P (shot two), the finger billiardist can make the cueball hug the rail until it curves into the side pocket. Shot three is one anybody can learn. With a sweeping motion of the hand (see dashed arrow), slap the top of the ball on the rail so that it rebounds from the rail and spins back into the side. (From Jim Mataya.)

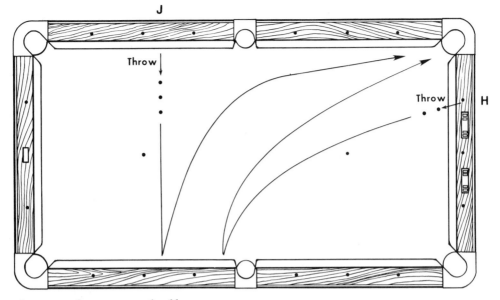

A sweeping curveball

Mike Massey can stand at H or at J and make the cueball bank once into the corner. I can't.

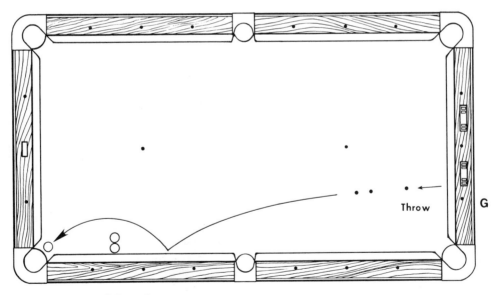

The out-and-in shot

Mike again. Standing at G, he spins the cueball down the table in such a way so that it banks around two balls sticking out from the rail. It's the damndest thing you ever saw.

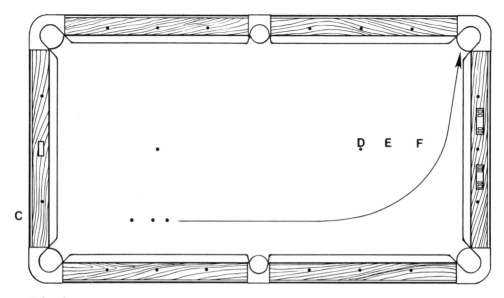

Limbo

Ever see anybody dance the Limbo? The dancer squeezes under a horizontal bar that is placed lower and lower. In the shot diagrammed here, Massey stands at C and throws the ball down the table. The object is to make it curve around an obstacle ball into the corner pocket. The obstacle is placed first at D, then E, then F, etc.

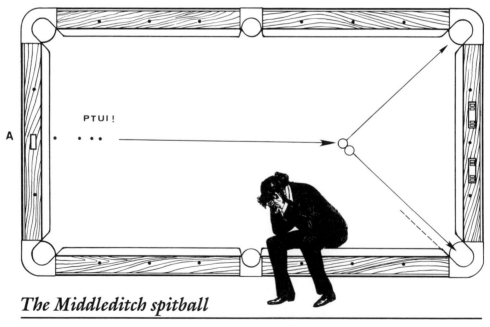

The Middleditch spitball

George Middleditch can stand at A and fire a ball from his mouth into two object balls, making them both. Once in a while an excessively prissy spectator will say, "Oh, how gross! I can't look!"

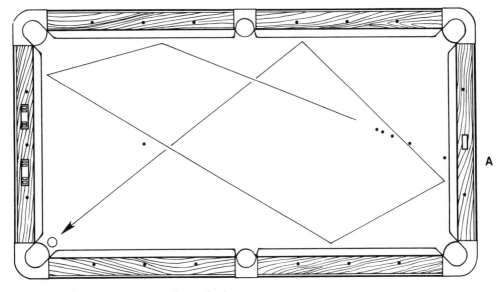

Steve Simpson's blowhard shot

People who have never lied to me swear that Steve Simpson can make a five-rail bank shot by shooting the ball from his mouth. I'd like to see it.

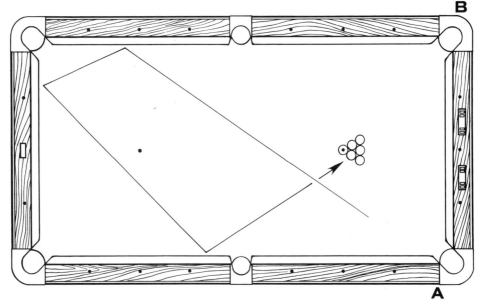

Finger billiards for all

You don't have to be an eccentric genius to have fun with finger billiards. If you have a table at home and your mother has ruined all the cues by using them to knock fruit from trees, try this game. Six balls are pyramided on the spot. Stand at A and by throwing the cueball, over and over, around the table as shown, see how long it takes to make all the balls in pocket B. Five minutes is good. Another game is to rack up all fifteen with the eight-ball buried in the center. Throwing the cueball three rails as before, try to make the eight in the corner in fewer tries than your opponent. Ten throws is excellent. With a cue, five shots is excellent. (From Bob Jewett.)

16
Showstoppers

Steve Mizerak showing off in the television commercial that made him famous.
(McCann Erickson)

W̲ant something wild, stunning, and unforgettable to close your show? Then take a look at the following diagrams. With the proper dramatic buildup, most of the shots in this chapter will provoke a noisy, tumultuous response from any audience not clinically dead. They're all tough, so stress that, and if you make every ball but one, knock it in with your cue. Don't make people suffer through a stretch of dead time while you laboriously reconstruct a complicated layout. Select the series of shots in your program with pacing as well as variety in mind. The secret of lasting success is to build to a climax and quit while they still want more.

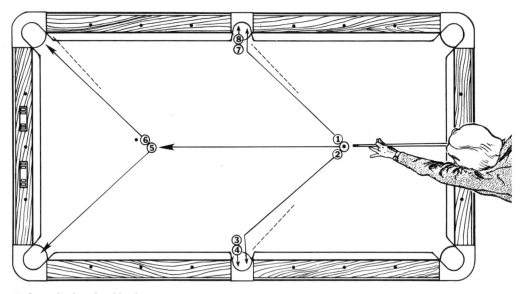

The eight-ball shot

This is a good closing shot because it isn't inordinately difficult and yet a lot of balls go in. Some credit it to Bill "Weenie Beenie" Staton, others to Don Tozer.

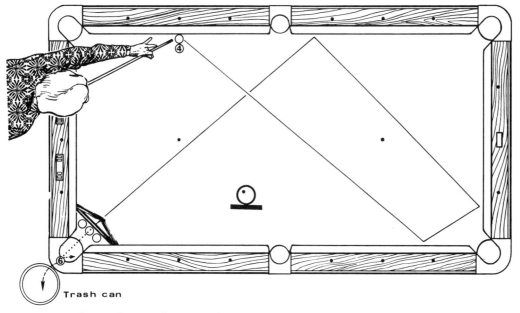

Trash can

Bucktooth Cook's trash-can shot

Put a trash can on the floor behind one corner pocket. The six-ball is on top of the pocket, held in place by a paper match or a piece of chalk. An upright triangle guards the pocket entrance. The outlandish idea is to make the cueball leap into the air, as it will do when it passes over the side of the triangle, knock the six into the can, and fall back into the pocket. The first part of the shot can be any number of things; escaping from behind the four by shooting into the rail is what Charles Cook suggests.

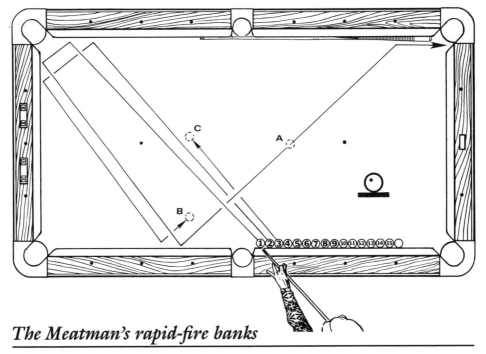

The Meatman's rapid-fire banks

Former world champion Joe Balsis is called the Meatman because he used to be a butcher. One of the highlights of his trick-shot show is a series of round-the-table banks executed at high speed. Note that a cue is against the upper long rail to guide errant balls into the corner pocket. The more balls there are in motion the more impressive is the shot. The diagram is intended to show that when the one is at A and the two is at B, the three is fired between them. A gulley table is needed; otherwise the corner pocket will become glutted with balls. The basic idea goes back to Anonymous.

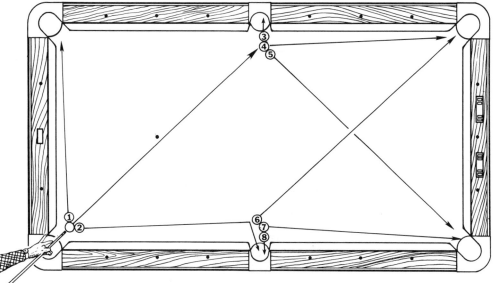

The every-which-way shot

A severe test of skill from Nicholl.

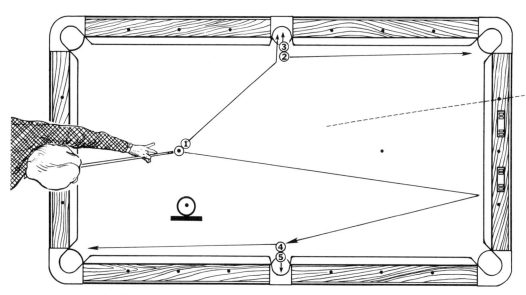

A five-ball eye-opener

Even if you can't make this shot, you probably can think of a better name for it. If you can hit the cueball with no English, then once you find the proper aiming point for your equipment the shot becomes slightly easier than it looks. Shown to me by Gerni.

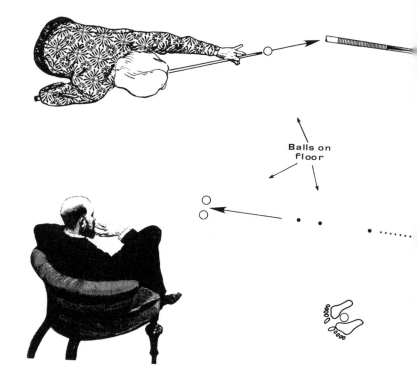

Balls on
floor

The rake's progress and the French backflip

There is a lot to be said for saving an easy shot for last. That way you can be sure of ending on a successful note instead of a discord. The audience will accept it if some humor is involved. In the diagram, note the chain of three cues. The one at the left angles downward from the corner of the table to the floor. By kneeling down and shooting a cueball into the butt of the rake, you can make a ball at A. Announce your intention before arranging the rakes.

At the 1978 World Three-Cushion Tournament at the Sahara Hotel in Las Vegas I saw Belgium's Ludo Dieles jump a cueball from the table and score a billiard on two balls trapped between the feet of Belgium's Raymond Ceulemans. (This was in a trick-shot show, not in a game.) That shot also is

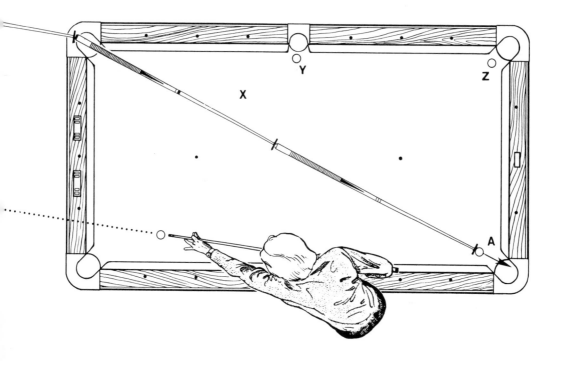

diagrammed. The Navarra brothers of Argentina, according to Blyth Adams, have a version of this in which the cueball goes through an open door and bounces down a flight of stairs to the sidewalk, where object balls await.

Speaking of feet, you may be wondering about the two bare ones. The owner of those feet, which can be shod, is going to jump in the air, bend his knees, and throw a ball *with his feet* onto the table so it lands at point X, from whence it will pocket balls at Y and Z. Do I hear snorts of disbelief? I almost made the shot myself on the second try. (On the first try the ball sailed all the way over the table and nearly broke the glass of a candy display case.) This was one of Captain Mingaud's greatest "shots" and is described in his 1827 book.

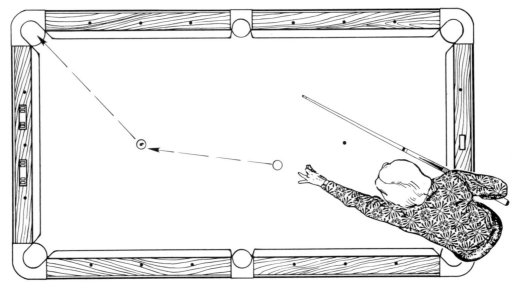

The Deacon's blind cut

Get set to cut a ball in off the spot. Before pulling the trigger, turn your head to one side, open your bridge-hand fingers to release the cue (but keep the bridge hand planted on the table), wave the cue in the air, carefully return the cue to the bridge hand, and, still without looking, cut the object ball into the corner. If you've grooved your aim at the beginning, the stunt is well within the realm of possibility. Irving "The Deacon" Crane thinks so highly of the shot that he often uses it as the climax of his show, with the object ball on the foot spot and the cueball on the head spot—that's a tough cut even with your eyes open.

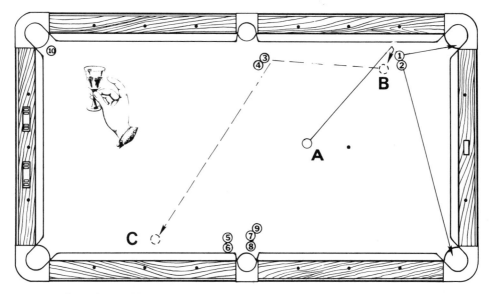

"Just showin' off . . ." complete

Here is the three-shot sequence that made Steve Mizerak famous. See how well the shots are planned to make it fairly easy to get the cueball from one to another. The one and two are made from cueball position A, the three and four from B, and the rest of the balls from C. The glass is lifted from the table just in time to let the cueball pass underneath. (The six-ball shot is detailed on page 5.) If you want to memorize Steve's lines as well as his shots, here they are: "When you play a lot of pool in bars, you want to stay fast and loose. You don't want to get filled up. That's why I drink Lite beer from Miller. It has a third less calories than their regular beer, and it's less filling. Plus, the taste is great. And even though a lot of people don't think pool is strenuous, let me tell you something. You can work up a real good thirst even when you're [pick up glass and smile] just showin' off."

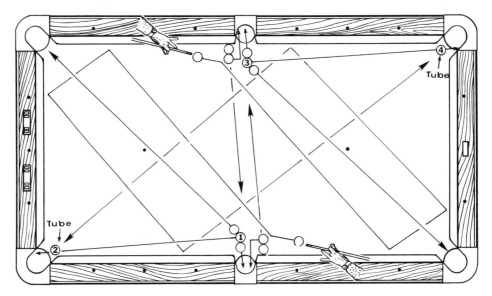

"Just showin' off . . ." double

A great curtain-closer is to shoot two "just showin' off" shots at once with the help of a cohort. Balls fly into pockets in all directions. For years it was assumed that you had to leave the sixth ball out of each cluster for reasons of interference, then Red Jones of Saint Petersburg, Florida, had the great idea of putting them on coin tubes. In the diagram, for example, the one-ball goes under the two. The two drops to the table, and is pocketed by the other player's cueball. The three and four are handled the same way.

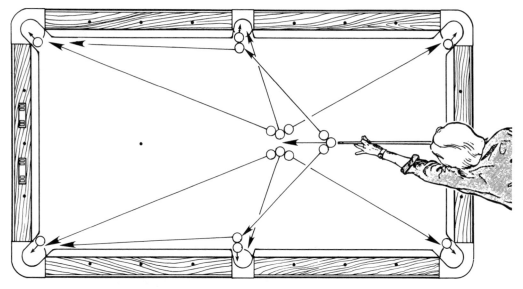

Sixteen balls at once

A lot of things have to work perfectly for all sixteen balls to drop. The concept is so audacious you will be applauded for your courage even if a ball or two remains in view at the end. Great care is needed in positioning the balls; for heaven's sakes, don't try to do it while people are fidgeting in their seats. If you can't set it up in advance, leave it out of your program. Bill "Weenie Beenie" Staton made the shot on Steve Allen's "I've Got a Secret" television show in 1967. Good old Anonymous in his 1918 book shows a fourteen-ball version, omitting the two balls frozen to the cueball.

The gravestone of Australian Walter Lindrum, twice world champion in English billiards, and his wife, Beryl. If Mrs. Lindrum was anything like the wives of many American players, she is as interested in the game now as she ever was.

BOOK TWO

BILLIARDS

Introduction

What can be done with only three balls and a table with no pockets? Wonderful things. On a billiard table you can make use of the entire length of the rails, including especially the corners. A standard billiard table has twenty-five percent more area than a standard pool table, giving the balls room to spread their wings. Distances and travel times are greater. Billiard cloth, especially that made by Simonis in Belgium and Gorina (the trade name is Granito) in Spain, is much smoother and finer than pool cloth, which means that the balls roll farther and spin longer. Blink and you'll miss seeing most pool shots; billiard shots last as long as ten or fifteen seconds.

Billiard trick-shot artists are scarce in the United States but plentiful in Europe, South America, and Japan, where billiards, not pool, is the main game. The Europeans are so enthralled by what they call "artistic" or "fantasy" billiards that they hold national and world tournaments in it every year. Americans who have taken the trouble to attend, like George Rippe of Salem, New Hampshire, the late Ed Smoker of Philadelphia, Pennsylvania, and Ely Castleman of Baltimore, Maryland, return stunned and raving about the spectacular feats they have seen.

In a tournament of artistic billiards, contestants get three tries to make seventy-six prescribed shots, scoring between four and eleven points for each success, depending on the rated difficulty of the shot. A sampling of the official tournament shots are scattered through the diagrams that follow, together with their difficulty ratings. If you want to see all seventy-six, send for Bob Jewett's collection of eight-by-ten drawings (see Bibliography). You may not believe some of the cueball paths. If you don't, go to Antwerp and ask for René Vingerhoedt or to Buenos Aires and ask for Ezequiel Navarra. They'll prove to you that I wasn't hallucinating when I made the diagrams. Dates of upcoming national, European, and world artistic billiard tournaments can be obtained by writing to Union Mondial Billard, c/o Lambert Carabin, Avenue de la Croix-Rouge 13/206, 4020 Liège, Belgium. Enclose a few International Reply Coupons, available at any post office, for the return postage.

Readers interested in billiards are also directed to *Byrne's Standard Book of Pool and Billiards,* which has more than two hundred diagrams of billiard shots, many of which are flashy enough to use in exhibitions.

As in Book One, I am including, for amusement purposes and to show what the great masters are capable of, some extremely difficult and high-hazard shots. My assumption is that the untrained will not be so foolish as to try them. If I'm wrong, may God have mercy on my soul.

1
Appetizers

Proprietors should put a stop to horseplay the moment it starts.
(Moldenhauer Collection)

A wide variety of shots to whet your appetite. In this chapter and the rest, watch for practical ideas you can use in games.

Otto Reiselt, three times world three-cushion champion, complained good-naturedly to Ripley in a letter that the cartoon should have shown a billiard table, not a pool table. The shot would look good today on television.

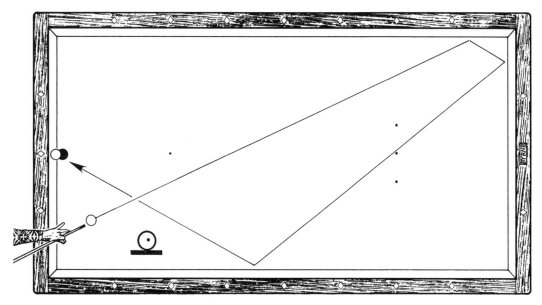

Charlie Peterson's topple shot

The white is on top of the rail, held in place by the red. The object is to make a three-cushion bank. Shoot very softly, so that when the cueball dislodges the red, the white will fall on it to complete the billiard.

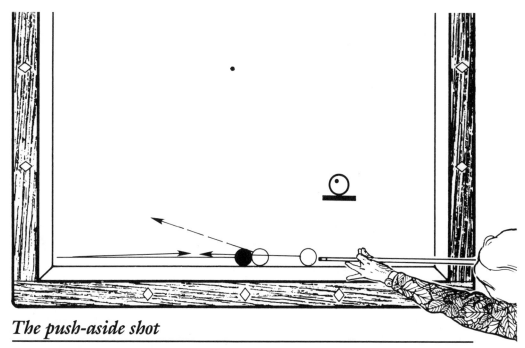

The push-aside shot

What's the best way to hit both object balls? By using left follow. The white gets bumped aside and the cueball goes forward to meet the returning red. (McCleery, 1890.)

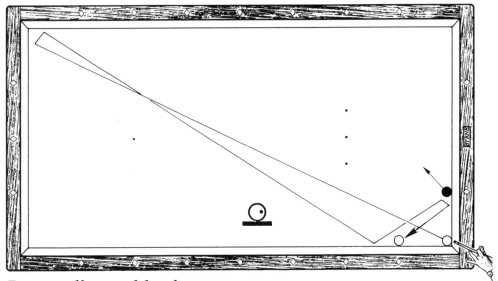

Reverse diagonal bank

The beautiful thing here is that the cueball *misses* the white off the third rail, hitting it after the red and the fourth rail. I learned it from Gus Copulus. Ernie Presto of Chicago credits it to Charlie Morin, who had a run of eighteen in 1915.

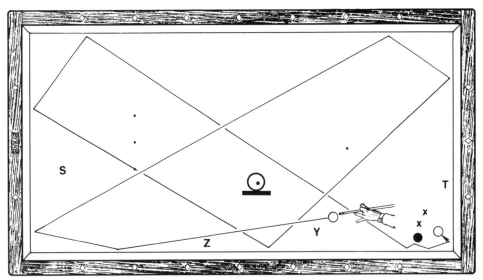

The ten-rail bank

Unless the cloth is new and the rails are fast, nine rails is the most you can hit without resorting to this trick, which Willie Hoppe often made a part of his exhibitions. The standard pattern is to place the two object balls at the x's. Hoppe placed them as shown, which results in an extra rail. Could Isidro Ribas of Spain hit ten rails by starting from S, shooting to T, banking to Z, etc.? That claim was published in 1928 by Robert Ripley in his "Believe It or Not" column. I don't believe it. (Hint to those trying the bank the normal way: Start at Z instead of Y and use slight low right.)

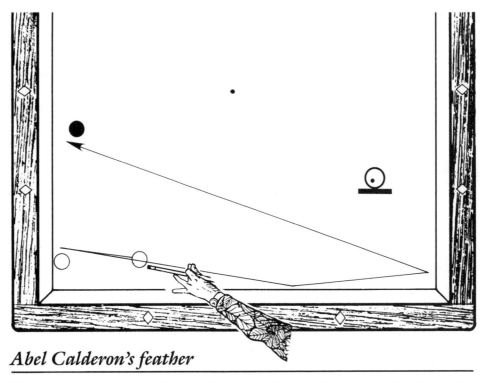

Abel Calderon's feather

The cueball and the white are the same distance from the end rail, yet it's possible to make a short angle shot off the white. (See page 146.)

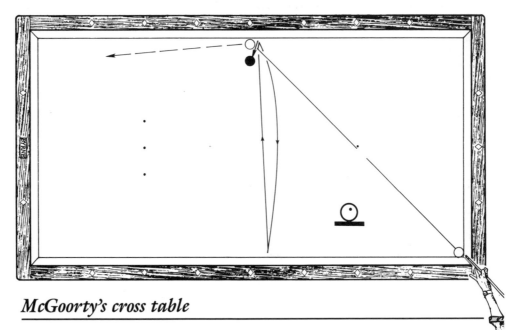

McGoorty's cross table

As unlikely as it seems, a cross-table shot can be made in this position. Danny McGoorty showed me the idea in 1965.

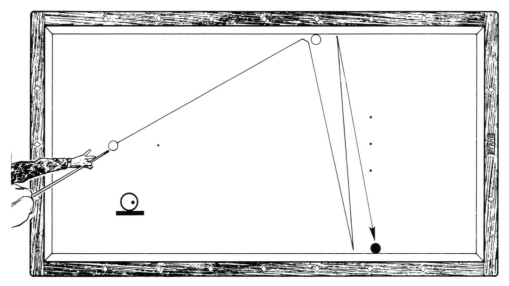

Harold Rooff's moment of glory

The lovely feature here is the way the reverse English acts off both the second and third rails. When Harold Rooff of New York City made the shot against Joe Chamaco in the 1950 National Tournament, Willie Hoppe stood up in the stands and led the applause.

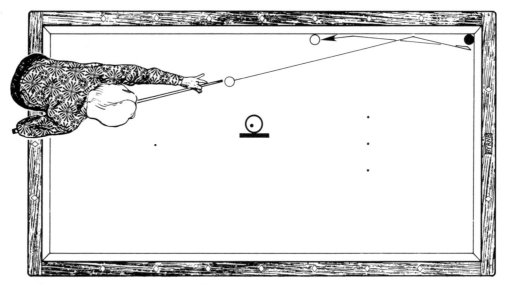

Whitey the Beer Salesman's shot

The title is taken from the nickname by which Jim McFarlane of Alameda, California, was once known. Shoot softly with maximum left spin. The cueball hits two rails, *then* the red ball.

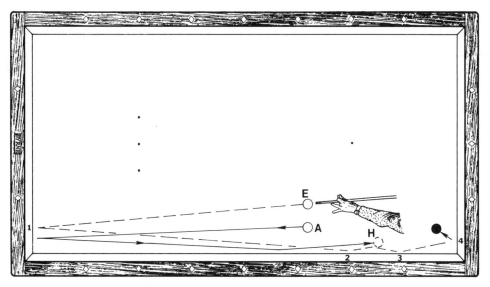

The running ticky

First shoot the A ball. Shoot the E ball a little faster so that it catches up to A near H. The E ball will contact the red after hitting three or four rails. (McCleery.)

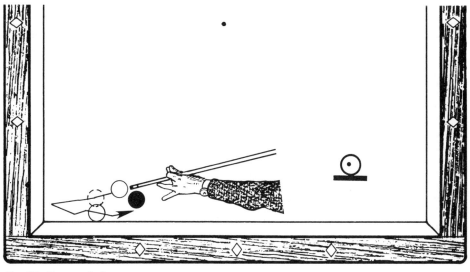

Ball-first ticky

The white is frozen on the rail. The cueball grazes it on the way to the side rail, bringing it away from the end rail to allow the returning cueball to get two more rails as it goes through the newly formed hole before contacting the red. In other words, the cueball follows this sequence: white, side rail, end rail, white again, end rail again, red. Shown to me by Bud Harris of San Francisco.

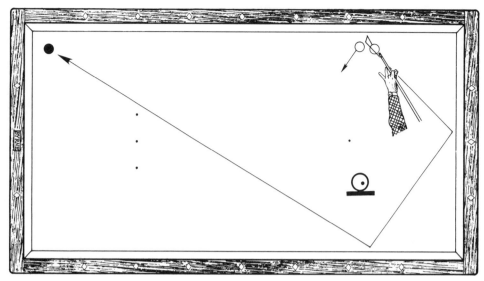

Mr. Norman Smith's shot

A certain kind of imagination is necessary to be a good three-cushion player. I knew Norm Smith of Novato, California, had it when as a raw student of the game he came up with this shot. Go into the rail with *right* English. Now you'll have three rails before approaching the big ball in the corner.

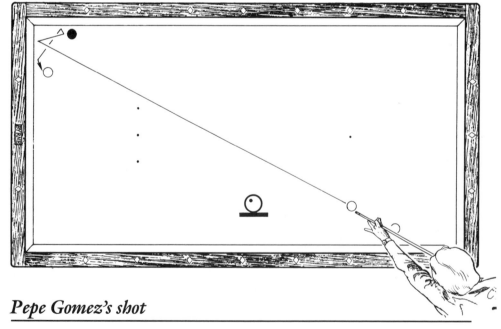

Pepe Gomez's shot

Pepe Gomez, who can be found at Tiff's North Hollywood Billiards, can make this and many other shots. After hitting the red with good speed, the cueball barely crawls to the white. Put the red closer to the end rail if you want to make it less impossible.

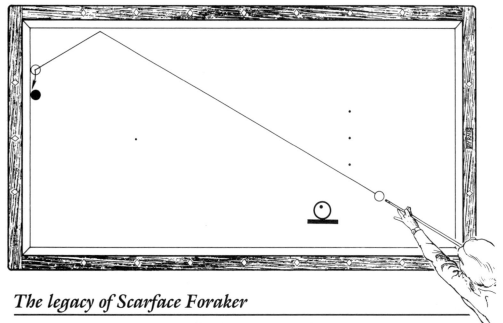

The legacy of Scarface Foraker

Scarface Foraker, who, I was told by McGoorty, was barred from several tournaments because he carried a gun, left us this incredible shot to remember him by. After going off the side rail, the cueball goes through the white to the end rail, then hits the end rail again before hitting the red. Don't try it in a game of three-cushion without coaching your opponent in advance.

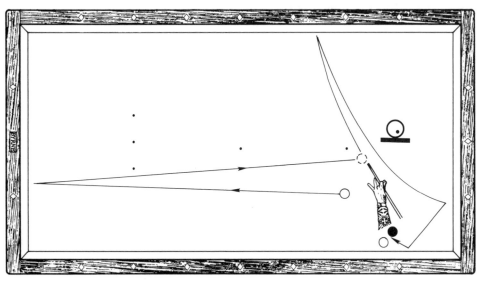

Double-stroke three-cushion shot

Very tough. Bank the cueball the length of the table, then reposition yourself so you can hit the returning cueball toward the side rail with low right. This shot, which is in McCleery's 1890 book, should keep Snooks Perlstein busy for another sixty years. (See page 194.)

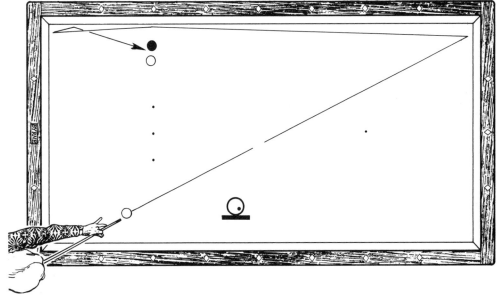

Maximum reverse

When a sketch of this shot arrived from Panama, I thought it might be possible only on some sort of weird jungle equipment. Wrong. I made it on the fourth try. Find a spot for the cueball so that maximum reverse sends it almost straight along the long rail. (Thank you, Señor Maduro.)

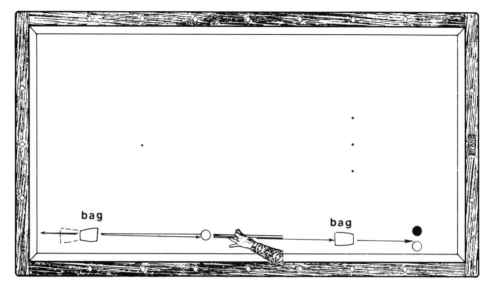

The Panamanian bag shot

From Panama's Guillermo "Mimo" Martinez comes this enchanting novelty, which is based on the well-known fact that a cueball rolling into a paper bag will make it flip over. Place two bags as diagrammed. The cueball is shot into the open mouth of the first bag, flipping it over, then rebounds from the rail and goes back into the same bag, flipping it over again. The cueball proceeds to the second bag, flipping it over, and scores a carom on the two object balls. Paul Gerni has found that the bag that flips most readily is the type whose wide sides converge to a line, or edge (popcorn or french-fry bags), rather than the type with a flat bottom. He also suggests a strip of double-stick tape to keep the bag from sliding.

2

Time Shots

Wherever the game is played you can find creeps and weirdos who
don't have jobs and who just hang around.
(Moldenhauer Collection)

In a time shot, all three balls are deliberately set in motion. The second object ball is sent to a new address, where the cueball must find it. Time shots are always greeted with applause, even though many of them are quite easy. You could almost put on a show with the shots in this chapter.

Ripley's —— Believe It or Not!®

CHAS. PETERSON – FAMOUS TRICK-SHOT BILLIARD STAR
RAN 20,000 POINTS AT STRAIGHT RAIL BILLIARDS IN 101 MINUTES, 8 SECONDS
HE SCORED 100 POINTS IN 22 SECONDS   CHICAGO, May - 1935
© RIPLEY INTERNATIONAL LIMITED 1935

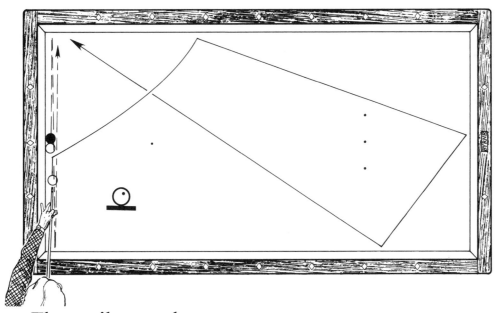

Three-rail natural

Hit the white fairly full. The cueball goes around the table in a natural pattern while the red banks twice across. (McCleery.)

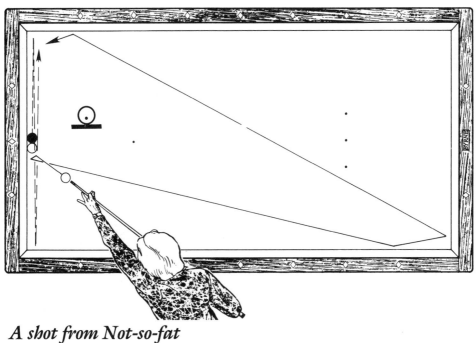

A shot from Not-so-fat

Again the red is driven twice across, but the cueball takes a long-angle path. From Harry "Not-so-fat" Sims.

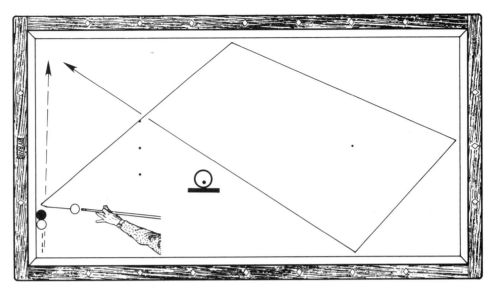

Four-rail natural

Self-explanatory. The first time you try it you'll probably hit the red too thick.

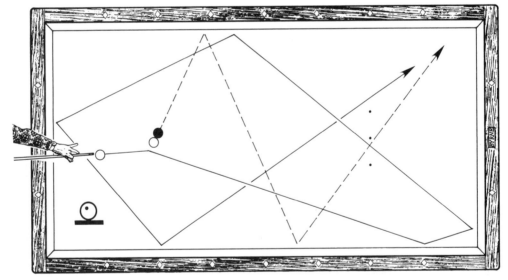

Five-rail natural

The red zig-zags to the corner, the cueball finds it after going five rails. A favorite exhibition shot of Welker Cochran, who dominated the game, and Hoppe, from 1927 to 1946.

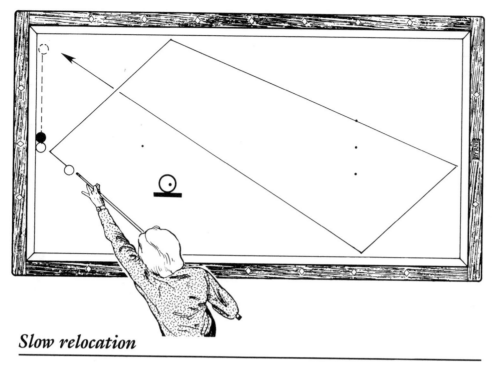

Slow relocation

This is nice because the red creeps slowly to the corner to wait for the cueball, which kisses back off the white. From Harry Sims.

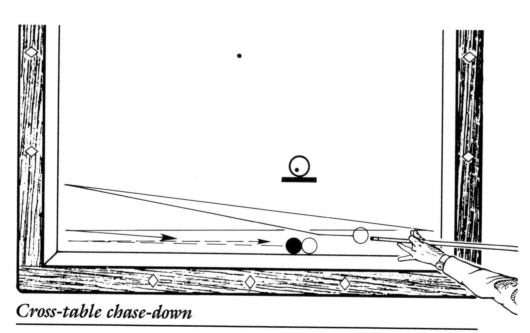

Cross-table chase-down

The idea here is that the shooter doesn't know where the red will be when the cueball finally catches up with it—it depends on how thinly the white is hit at the start. A favorite of America's premier player, Al Gilbert of Hollywood, California.

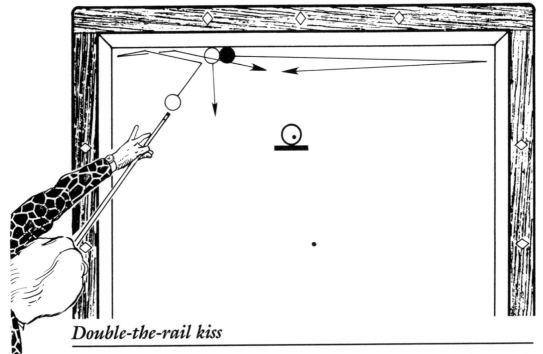

Double-the-rail kiss

Draw action is easy to get when the object ball is frozen to another. Don't shoot hard. A shot from Jimmy Lee's bottomless bag of tricks. At eighty-four years of age, Jimmy can be found at the Palace Billiards in San Francisco every night of the year except one. He stays home for the Miss America Pageant.

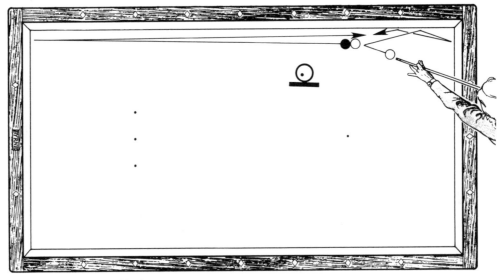

Double-the-rail draw

Not quite as easy as the previous shot. Shown to me by Nabih Yousri, many time champion of Egypt and the man who drove Omar Sharif out of billiards and into acting.

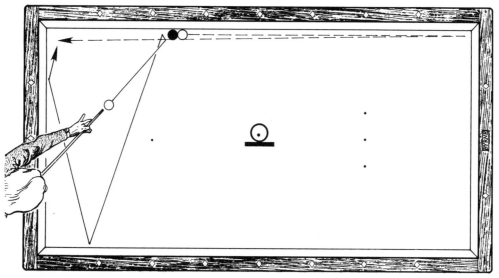

Cross-table rendezvous

From McCleery's 1890 book.

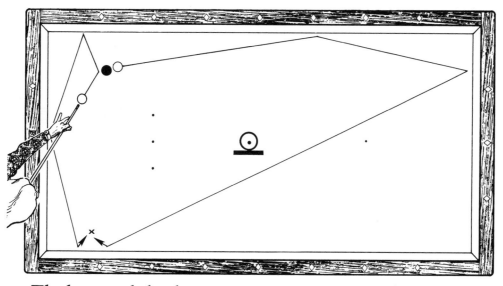

The long and the short

Pete Dekker, one of Holland's best players, demonstrated this on a 1981 tour of the San Francisco Bay Area. The cueball travels slowly and should be almost dead when the white ball meets it.

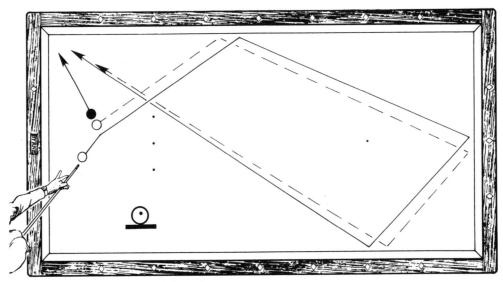

Dekker's double-time shot

An unusual shot from Pete Dekker. The idea is to make two three-cushion billiards with two strokes. First hit the white as shown, sending the red ball into the corner. Now shoot the white around the table so that it catches up to the cueball and hits the red as well for the second point. Because of the multiple possibilities, the shot is not quite as hard as it looks. One key is to hit the white thinly on the first cueball stroke so that it stays put, simplifying the second stroke. Rephrased, the first point is scored when the cueball catches up to the red in the corner; the second is scored when the white hits both the other balls in the corner.

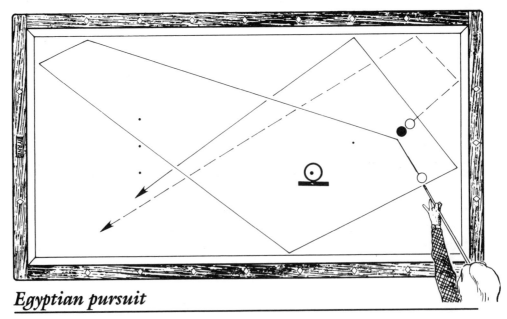

Egyptian pursuit

After going five rails off the red, the cueball pursues the white into the corner, usually catching it. Shown by Nabih Yousri.

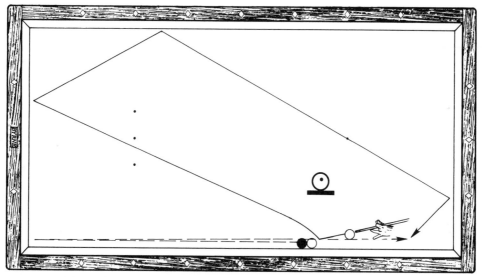

Something from Willie Hoppe

Hoppe often included this in his program of exhibition shots.

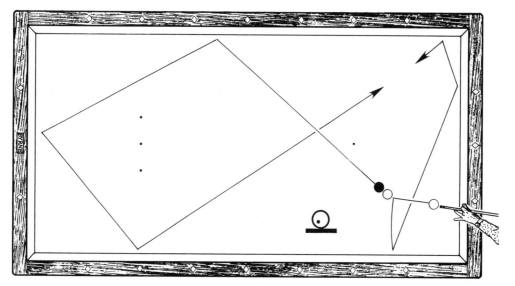

Dudley Kavanaugh's shot

John A. Thatcher, in his 1898 book, credits this to Dudley Kavanaugh. You remember Dudley. He won the 1863 tournament, the first ever held in the United States.

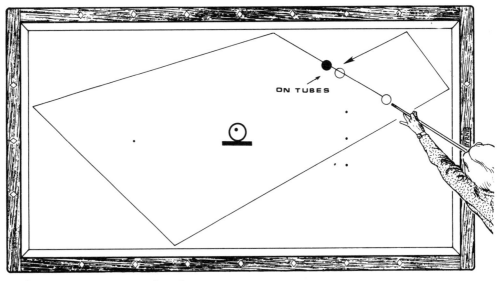

Johnny Layton's tube shot

I have a film of the great Johnny Layton shooting this before the start of the 1936 World Billiard Tournament. When the cueball knocks the paper tubes out from under the object balls, the balls drop straight down and wait for the return of the cueball. For other ideas involving tubes that could be adapted to billiards, see Book One, Chapter Eight.

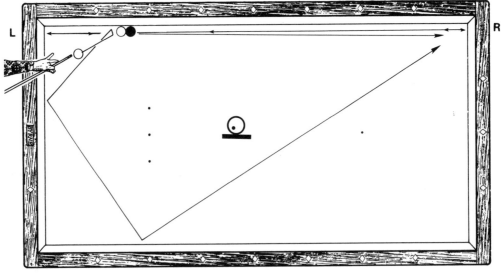

Victor Maduro's time shot

The red ball meets the cueball after traveling three lengths of the table—to R, to L, and back to R.

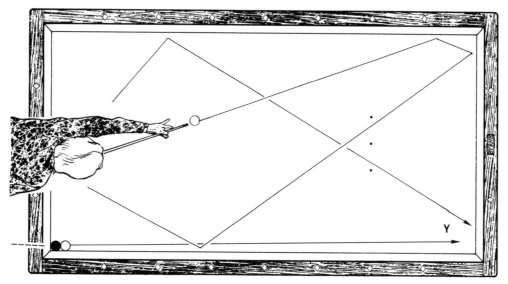

Two-stroke time shot

After launching the cueball on a five-rail path to Y, coolly walk to the bottom of the table, bridge over the white (as on p. 119), and shoot the red into the cushion, aiming along the dotted line. That will make the white ball kick back along the rail to meet the cueball . . . if your timing is right. A great crowd-pleaser and much easier than the old Charlie Peterson version that required a full massé on the second stroke. (From Victor Maduro.)

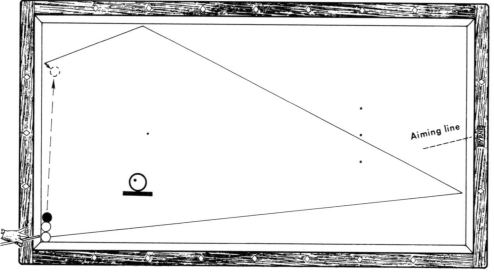

Deep freeze

Freeze three balls in the corner, but leave a one-eighth-inch space between the red and the rail. Aim at the nameplate and you'll make or come close to making a three-rail time shot almost every time. (Original.)

3

Kiss Shots

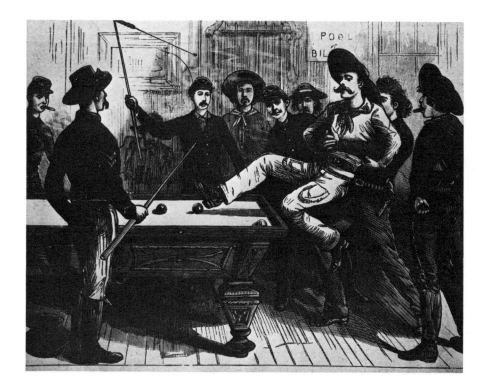

A game at odds between the cowboys and the cavalry, circa 1885.
(Billiard Archives)

Unsophisticated audiences give kiss shots a bigger response than they properly deserve, for some of them aren't difficult at all. Others are such low-percentage shots it would be madness even for champions to try them in public. They are fun to fool around with, though, after the joint closes.

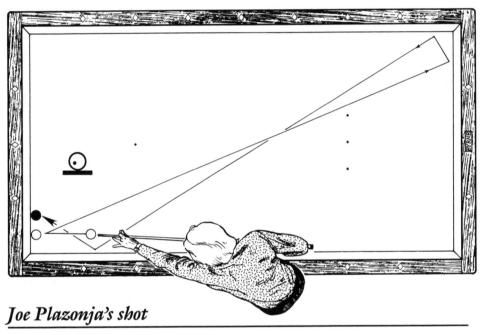

Joe Plazonja's shot

Because of his job, Joe Plazonja of Stamford, Connecticut, has lived all over the world, enabling him to learn a little about the art, language, and trick shots of many nations. Diagrammed is something he managed to pick up in Mexico.

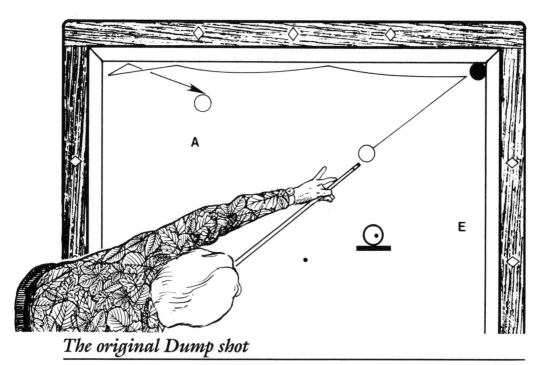

The original Dump shot

Beautiful hugging action, and not too difficult. Every billiard player should have it in his or her repertoire. Can be extended to a ball at E. With left English, which makes the shot tougher, the cueball will spin out of the corner to a ball at A. Credited by Thatcher in 1898 to somebody named Henry "Dump" Rhines.

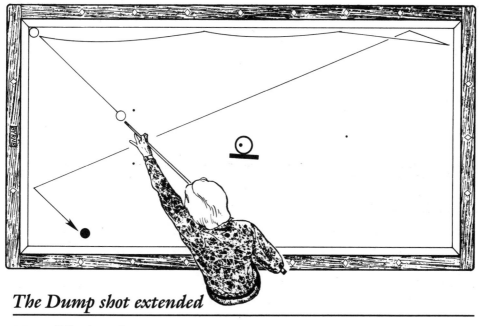

The Dump shot extended

More difficult and more spectacular than the previous pattern. A favorite of Nabih "The Curse of the Pharaohs" Yousri.

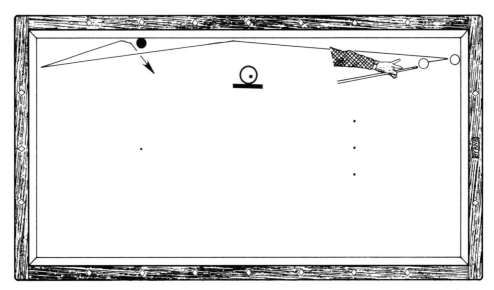

Long rail kiss-back

A three-cushion shot that anybody can make once in a while.

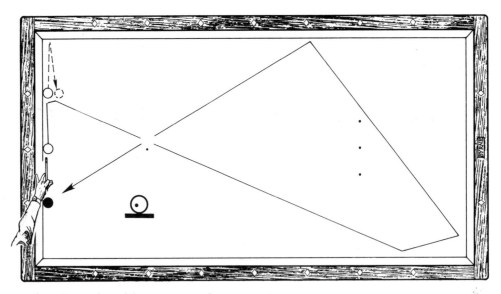

The Copulus kiss-around

Aim slightly into the rail with low left and shoot fairly hard. The point is to get a kiss at the location of the dashed ball, which will send the cueball around the table as diagrammed. I saw Gus Copulus make this shot in March of 1977 at 401 South Main in Los Angeles when he was eighty-four years old. (The shot is easier with the object balls closer to the corners.)

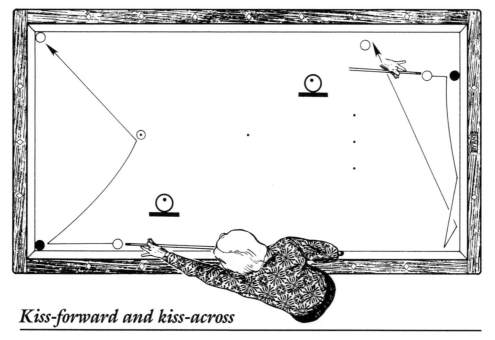

Kiss-forward and kiss-across

The four-ball shot at the left is from McCleery. See also page 29. The shot at the right is credited by Thatcher to a Parker Byers.

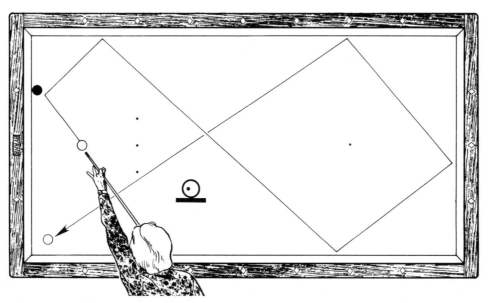

Reverse kiss-around

Here's one from the world tournament in artistic billiards sponsored every year by the Brussels-headquartered World Union of Billiards. In the scoring system used in that tournament, the shot is given a difficulty factor of four (on a scale of eleven), meaning that it is one of easiest of the seventy-six compulsory shots on the program. It's not easy at all, as you will discover if you try it. Could easily be adapted to pool.

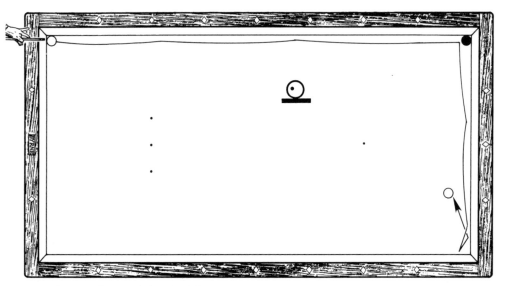

Arthur Thurnblad's kiss

Elevate your cue slightly and use maximum left English. Don't shoot too hard. Kiss through the hole, double the rail, and get a thrill you won't forget. Chicago's Billy Smith showed me this great shot in April of 1981 at the Denver Athletic Club. He learned it from Ernie Presto, who got it from Arthur Thurnblad in 1932.

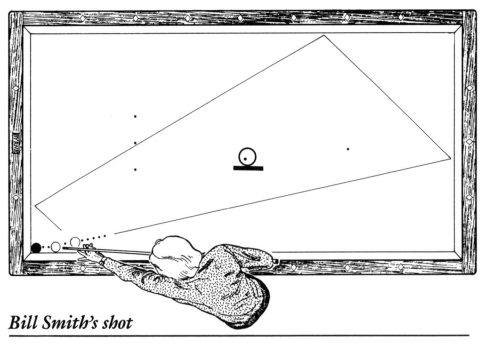

Bill Smith's shot

A good Smith invention and not hard to do. Elevate, use left English, and shoot fairly hard into the red. The cueball can be made to jump over the white and go around the table to score.

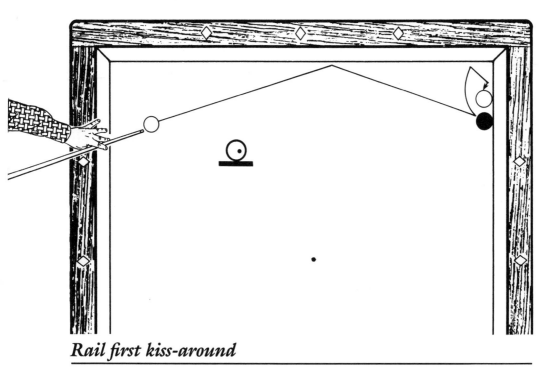

Rail first kiss-around

An extremely difficult test from Ernie Presto via Billy Smith. Related to the shots on page 252. A very soft touch is essential; the cueball should be barely moving when it spins off the third rail.

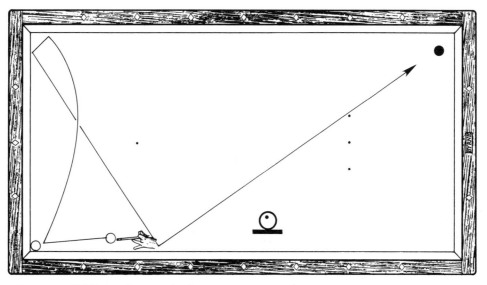

Byron Gillette's specialty

I don't know who Byron Gillette was, but Thatcher says this was one of his shots. In the artistic billiard tournament it's given a value of eight, which means that even the Europeans dread it.

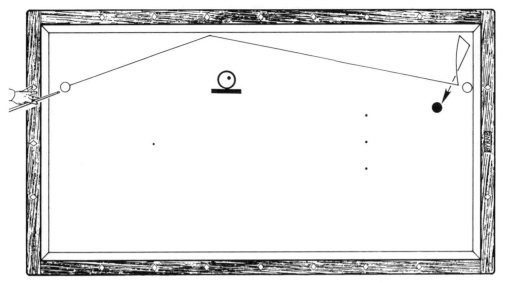

A Jimmy Lee shot

An impossible-looking shot from San Francisco's Jimmy Lee. You must kiss off the white to the *side* rail; if that happens the cueball will spin out of the corner and score. Careful control of speed is essential.

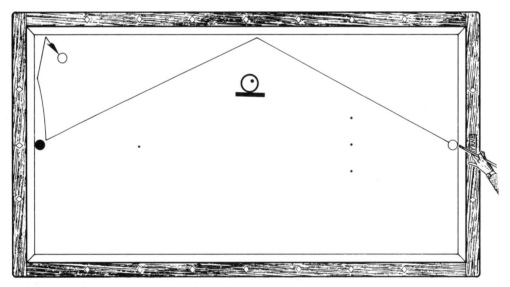

Something even worse

You thought the last shot was tough? Look at this one, also from Jimmy Lee. To have a chance of scoring, the cueball must be moving very slowly with plenty of spin after it kisses off the red. Try it at first without the cueball frozen and with the red closer to the white.

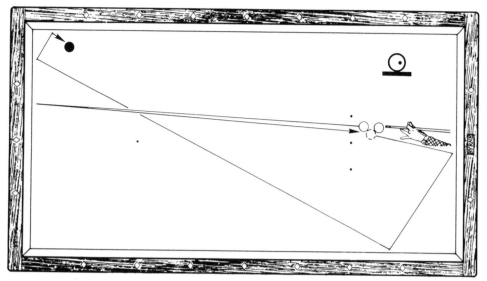

Wayman C. McCreery's shot

The monster on page 193 probably arose from this shot, which Thatcher credits to one Wayman C. McCreery. The cueball after hitting the white is left spinning in place. The white returns to send it on the diagrammed path.

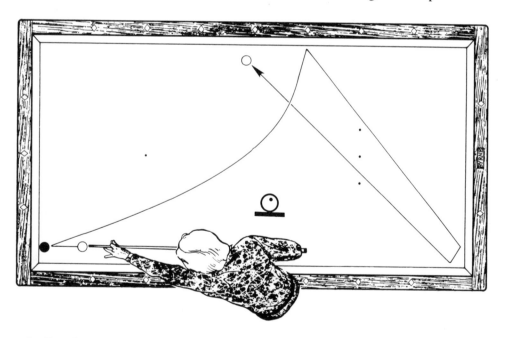

A Ceulemans killer kiss

In San Francisco's Chinatown in May of 1978, Raymond Ceulemans sketched this shot on a paper napkin, saying he "makes it sometimes at home." If he can make it only sometimes, the rest of us might as well not even try. (See next diagram.)

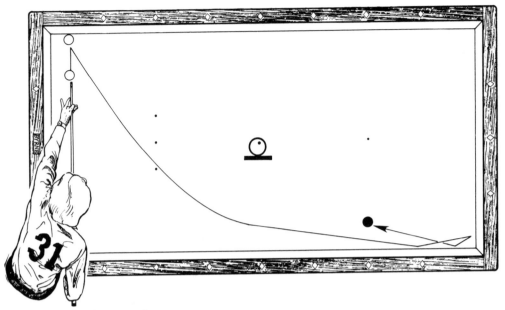

The ski-jump shot

Jimmy Lee grabbed the same napkin and sketched this shot. Ceulemans nodded enthusiastically and said *"Jawohl,"* which is German for "far out." By the time we left the restaurant, every napkin in the place was covered with circles and lines. The number thirty-one in the diagram has no significance; I just get tired of wearing my good shirts all the time.

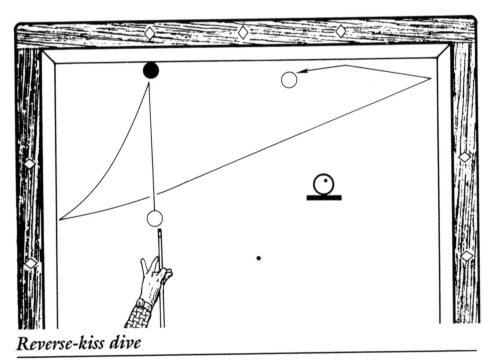

Reverse-kiss dive

Invented by Bill Smith. The English is reverse on all three rails.

4
Jump Shots

Paul Kerkau of Germany jumps a ball over a hat in 1906.

Making the cueball leave the table temporarily is perfectly legal provided you do it by striking it with a downward blow. Chip shots are okay in golf; not in pool or billiards. The angle of the cue to the horizontal should be between twenty and forty degrees for most jump shots; more than fifty degrees and the cueball might not be able to get out of the way of the descending cuetip and will stay on the cloth, which is what happens on a massé shot. Practicing jump shots is very hard on the equipment. Every stroke hammers a small pit into the cloth and there is the constant danger that an overzealous ball will leave the playing field entirely and break a window or a kneecap. Of the ten examples in this chapter, the first six could conceivably be tried in a game of three-cushion.

Ripley's—**Believe It or Not!**

SPENCER LIVSEY
– Pacific Coast cue star
EXECUTES ONE SHOT
ON TWO TABLES

THE CUE-BALL STRIKES AN OBJECT BALL AND THEN
HOPS TO THE SECOND TABLE – *GOING TWICE AROUND*
STRIKING *SEVEN* CUSHIONS AND TRAVELING A DISTANCE OF
48 FEET TO COMPLETE THE BILLIARD

© RIPLEY INTERNATIONAL LIMITED 1932

While this is a billiard shot, Livsey used to make it on two 6 × 12-ft. snooker tables.

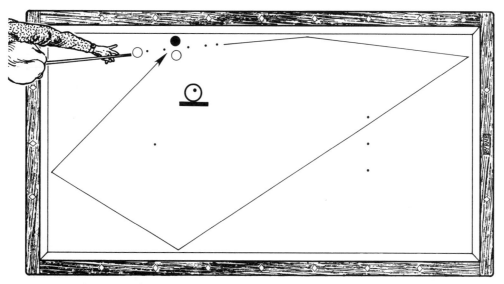

N. Lederer's shot

A jump shot will get the cueball through a space too small for it. Thatcher credits the shot to N. Lederer.

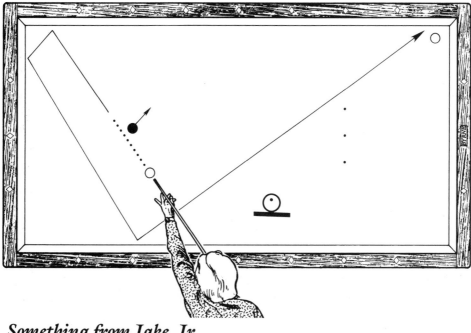

Something from Jake, Jr.

Let's assume you have a good three-cushion shot off the red but that you are afraid you can't hit it thinly enough. If the cueball is off the cloth when it passes the red, there is no problem with the thin hit. Jake Schaefer, Jr., gave Ernie Presto this tip in 1945. No English.

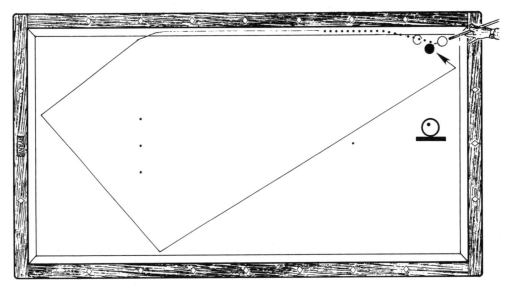

Rippe rides the rail

George Rippe loves this shot, which dates back far beyond his infancy. Jump over the red, ride the rail halfway down the table, then fall back to the bed and continue around the table to score. It's a legal shot if the cueball doesn't touch the wood. As a show shot, a little wood adds flavor. At George's Golden Cue in Lawrence, Massachusetts, one of the billiard tables is reserved for trick-shot practice.

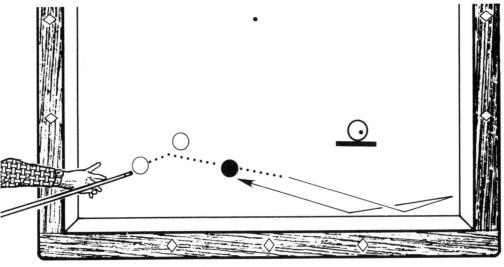

Jump double-the-rail

Hit the white, jump over the red, hit three rails in the corner, and return to score on the red. Bob Jewett thought of the idea in the summer of 1981 and furnished me with a sketch. When he reads this he'll discover that Jake Schaefer, Sr., often called The Wizard, beat him to it. Thatcher gives us the exact date: December 19, 1897.

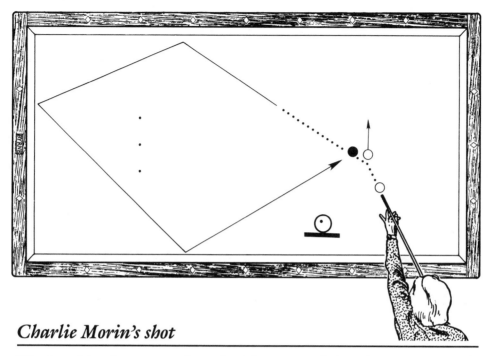

Charlie Morin's shot

Hit the white, jump over the red, and go around the table. Charlie Morin showed the shot to Ernie Presto in 1933.

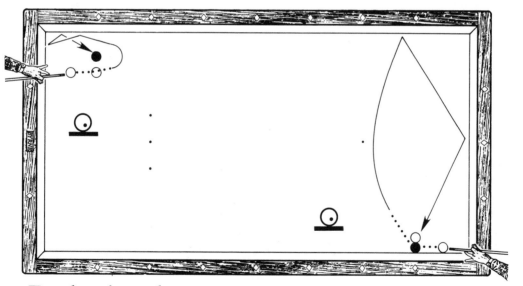

Two short jump draws

These two shots are from the artistic-billiard-tournament program and are rated as medium difficult. At the upper left, the jump stroke is needed to get the cueball past the first object ball before the draw takes effect. The shot at the lower right could be the basis of a good pool trick shot.

A long jump draw

Not so tough if you have a pile-driver, sledgehammer, King Kong, lightning-bolt stroke. This four-cushion shot rates the highest difficulty factor of eleven.

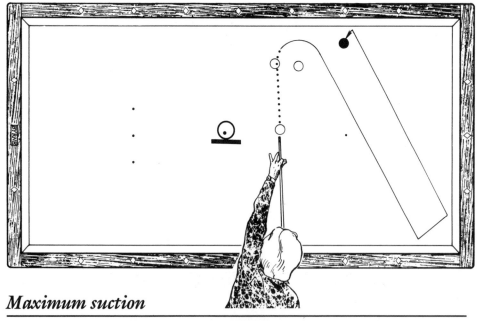

Maximum suction

There was a time when Zeke Navarra of Argentina was one of the few people who could execute this brutal shot. Now it is one of the compulsory figures at the world tournament and is considered one of the easiest shots in the competition. I can't think of six people in the United States who could make it. It's a little easier with the ivory balls they use at the tournament.

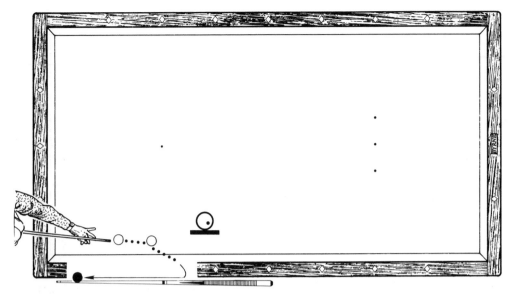

Knock on wood

Señor Maduro reminded me of this shot, which I have seen made by Juan Navarra and the Great Gargani, both of Argentina. Have a friend hold a cue along the outer edge of the rail with a ball at one end. Jump the cueball onto the wood with draw and right English. The spin acting on the cue will make the cueball creep along the rail until it contacts the red.

Bud Harris's jump

Shoot just hard enough to jump over the two object balls. San Francisco's Bud Harris, the inventor, points out that it would be perfectly legal in a game of three-cushion.

5

Draw Shots

Belgium's Raymond Ceulemans, the greatest billiard player of all time, in Buenos Aires in 1972 after winning one of his 100 major titles.

Groom your tip properly, chalk it well, hold the cue firmly, hit the cueball as low as possible, follow straight through, use enough speed, and you'll be able to make some of the eleven tough shots in this chapter. If you can't get good draw action on your cueball, take a lesson from someone who can.

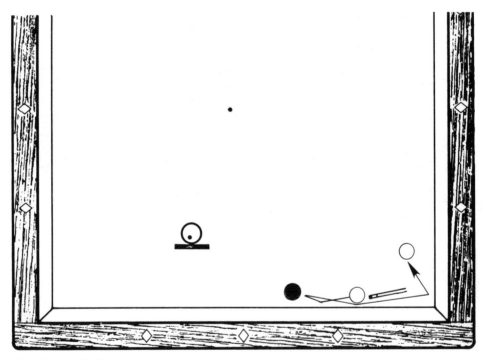

Bud's rail-first draw

Bud Harris made this against me in a game. Hit the rail first, then the red, and draw back to get two more rails in the corner.

The Wizard's double draw

With enough backspin the cueball will hit the end rail twice. Credited by Thatcher to Jake "The Wizard" Schaefer.

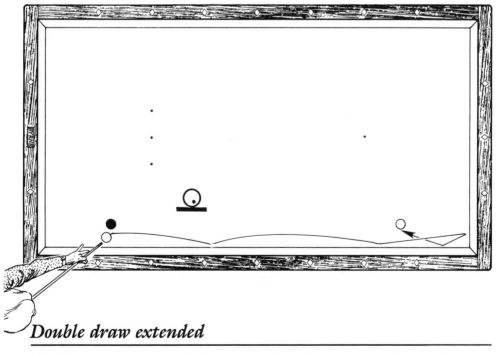

Double draw extended

The double draw again, with a twist at the end. A very well-known shot, also credited to Jake Schaefer, Sr.

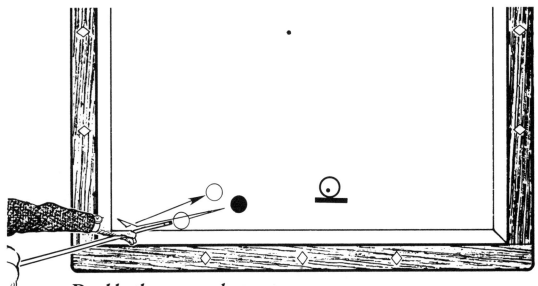

Double-the-corner draw

Even though the cueball is frozen to the rail, it's possible to get enough low left on it to draw back and get three rails in the corner. Shown to me by Eddie Robin.

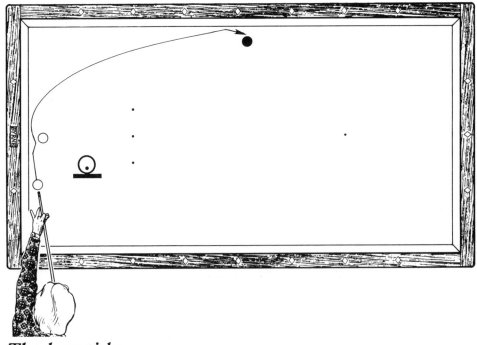

The draw ticky

Every top player knows that with draw you can make three-cushion shots like this, but how many know that Byron Gillette was shooting it a century ago?

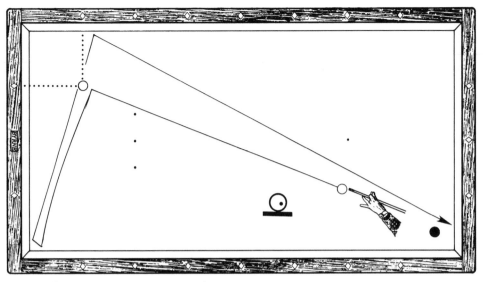

A Zeke Navarra natural

Test your stroke with this draw shot. Zeke Navarra claims that this is duck soup. The dotted lines show where to spot the object ball.

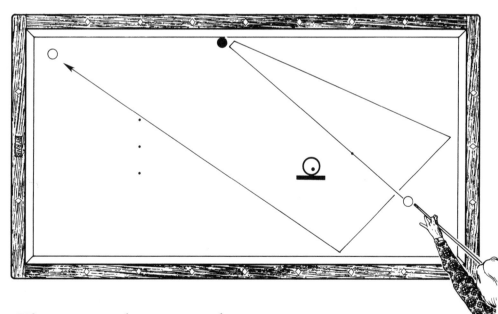

The greatest shot ever made

Thatcher went wild over this shot in the 1890s when he saw Professor Kaarless, the Belgian fancy-shot expert, make it, and he called it the greatest shot ever made. It's a standard shot now for the big strokers, and is on the world tournament program. Difficulty rating: eleven, which means don't even think about trying.

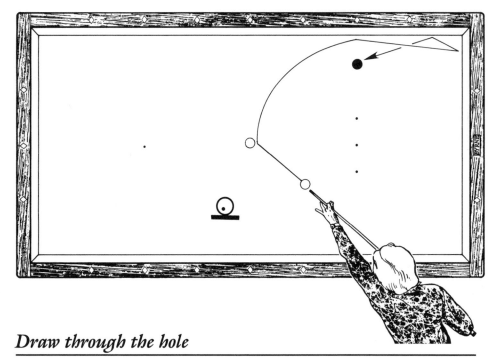

Draw through the hole

The Europeans give this a difficulty rating of eight. At a tournament in Oak Park, Michigan, a few years ago, I saw Bob Ameen make it on television.

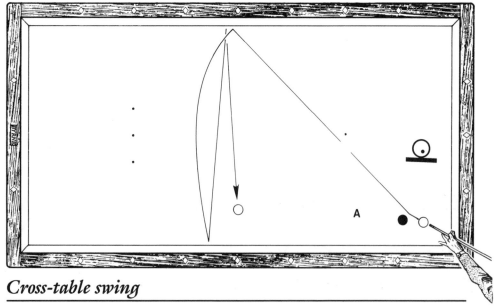

Cross-table swing

The European exhibition players think this is relatively easy and give it a rating of only six. It's not out of the question when the second object ball is at, say, A, where it was one night when Al Gilbert made the shot against me in North Hollywood.

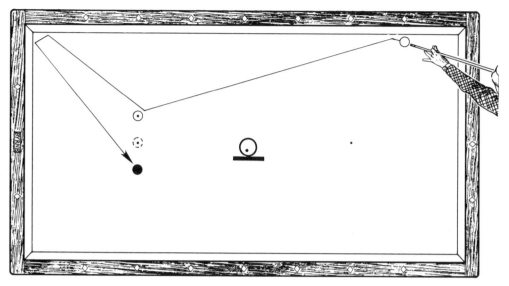

The idiotic ticky

Don't laugh—a ticky is possible from this position with maximum draw. It can even be made if the first object ball is on the spot (dashed ball). In practicing it, put the cueball in the same place each time and vary your aim by watching where the cue shaft crosses the end rail.

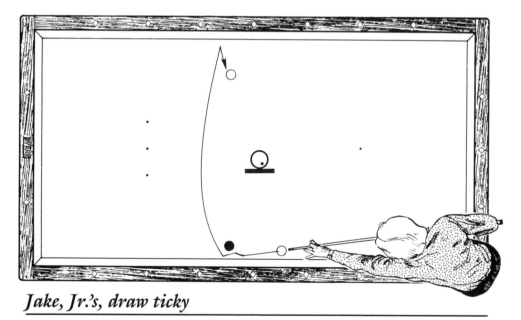

Jake, Jr.'s, draw ticky

According to retired cuemaker Harvey Martin, now in his nineties, this was a favorite shot of Jake Schaefer, Jr.

6
Follow Shots

A neat trick: Masako Katsura at the Palace Billiards in San Francisco in 1976. After a ten-year layoff, she picked up a borrowed cue and easily ran 100 points in straight billiards, a game in which her high run is an almost incredible 10,000.
Asleep behind her is your author.

There are more than 200 million people in the United States, and all but a few thousand of them are unable to put much spin on a cueball. What holds them back, I think—in addition to a lack of talent and interest—is the fear of the miscue that is apt to result from an off-center hit. The risk is worth taking. A miscue is embarrassing, but it doesn't begin to compare with the euphoria that accompanies a lively cueball. You want action? Then get that cuetip at least halfway out to the edge of the ball, use plenty of chalk, and follow straight through. Do those things and the beautiful follow shots in this chapter will be within your grasp.

Hug the rail

It's remarkable how small the hole can be between the white ball and the rail. The angle of approach to the red ball can be up to forty-five degrees. Shoot crisply and the cueball stays close to the rail. From Jimmy Lee.

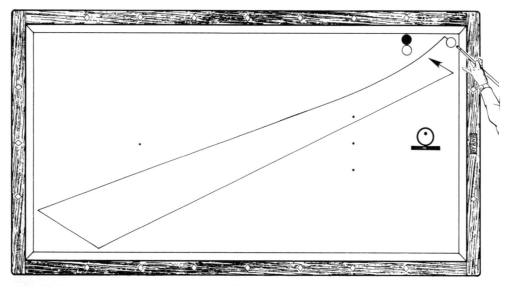

Bulldog Brink bends the ball

Top spin here enables the cueball to curve around the object balls. The diagrammed path results from a soft stroke; shoot more firmly and the cueball will hit closer to the corner and will approach the object balls on the "short" side. From Don Brink of Raytown, Missouri.

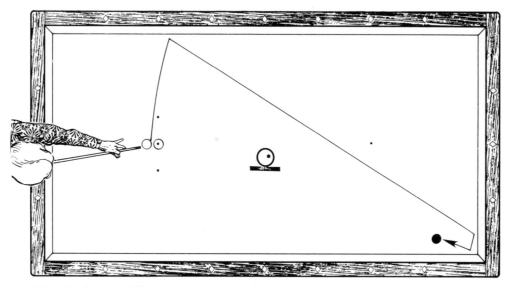

Basic force follow

The cueball is about a quarter inch from the object ball. Follow straight through with maximum right. Angle the line of aim just enough to miss the foul.

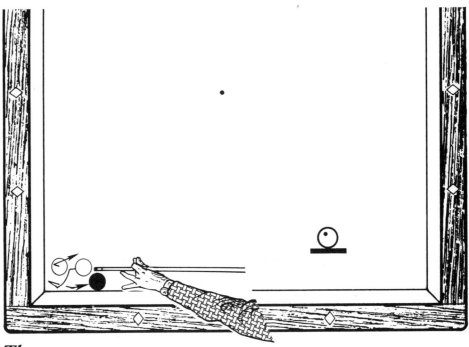

The cozy corner

Looks absolutely impossible. The secret is a soft stroke that gives the cueball time to bend forward into a feasible double-the-rail path. When it works, the red ball is bumped no more than half an inch. Shown to me by Eddie Robin.

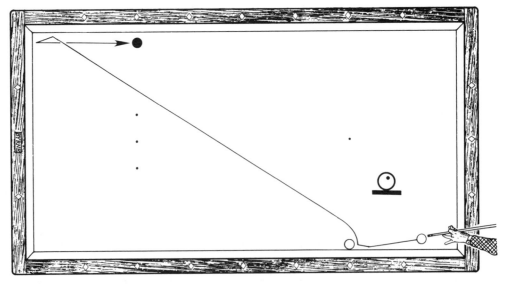

Rail first follow

A rail-first follow shot in this position is usually overlooked by three-cushion players. This shot is one of the easiest in the world artistic billiard competition.

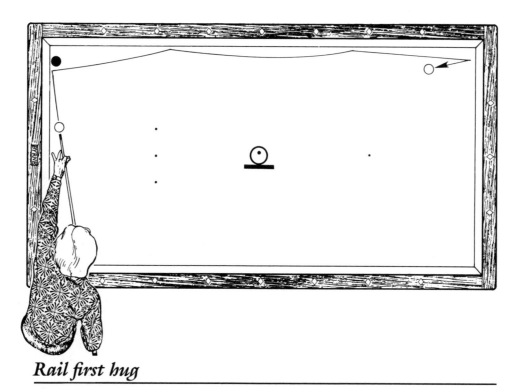

Rail first hug

Don't hit the red too full or it will kiss the cueball away. By hitting the rail first, the other object ball becomes a big target.

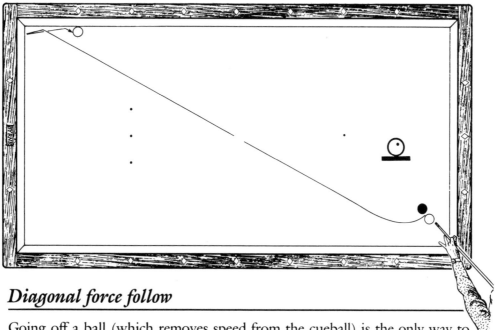

Diagonal force follow

Going off a ball (which removes speed from the cueball) is the only way to double the rail at this angle. Shown by Gus Copulus.

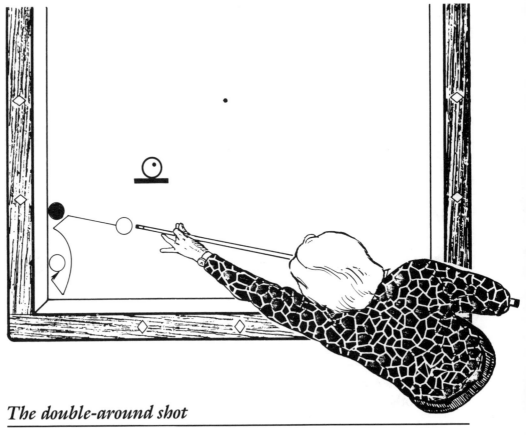

The double-around shot

To get three rails when the white is so close to the corner, the cueball must be spinning furiously when it hits the end rail. Credited by Thatcher to Eugene Carter.

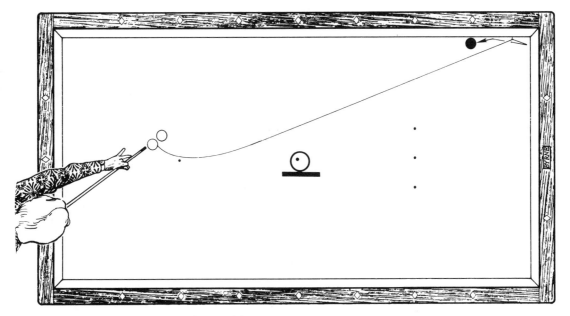

Curved double-the-rail

By taking advantage of the way the cueball curves on a force-follow shot, the rail can be doubled from a seemingly impossible position, though not very often. Dreamed up by George Rippe.

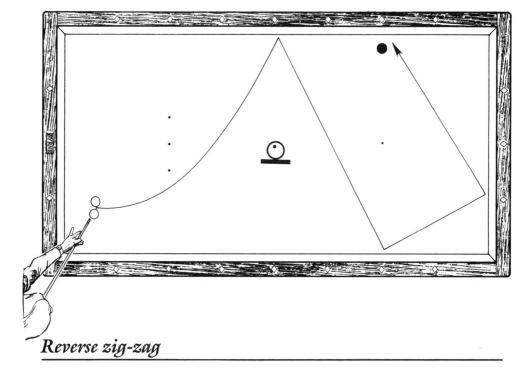

Reverse zig-zag

The cueball dives into the first rail, where most of its speed is lost because of the reverse English. If it manages to reach the second rail, spin will carry it the rest of the way. Difficulty factor in the world tournament: eight.

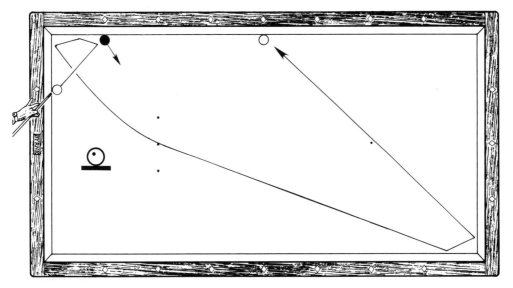

Follow stroke shot

Hit the red seven-eighths full with a powerful follow stroke and your cueball might trace the diagrammed path. Presto and Smith suggest high left, Bud Harris high alone. The origin of the shot is in dispute; that it isn't easy is agreed.

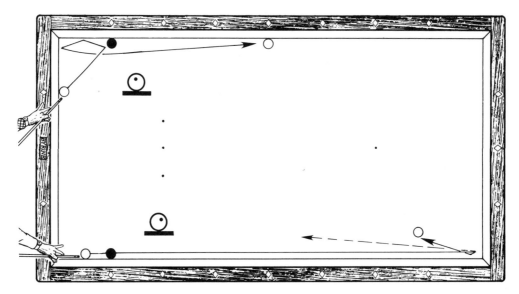

Two from Chicago

If you overwhelm the previous shot, the cueball sometimes dives back to the rail as shown at the top. Shown to me by Smith. The beautiful shot at the bottom was shown to Presto by Mexico's Joe Chamaco in 1941. Hit the red straight ahead with high right. The red will diverge from the side rail on the way back, allowing space for the cueball to pass and double the rail. Before drawing the diagram I made it four times in a row, which gives you an idea of its simplicity.

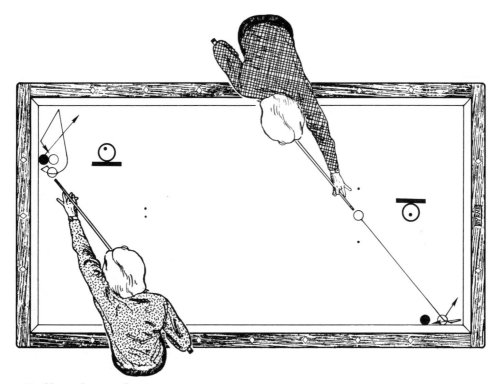

Follow into the corner

The pattern at the upper left is hard to achieve, especially with the cueball so close to the red, but a lot of players can do it. You must elevate the cue to get enough stuff on the ball. At the lower right, not much speed is needed and no English. Because the white is so close to the corner, follow alone does the trick.

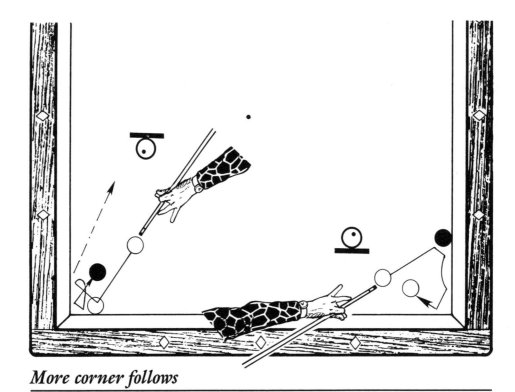

More corner follows

The three-cushion shot at the right is relatively easy. At the left, the white is banked through the hole with a powerful follow stroke. The cueball keeps fighting into the corner until after four, five, or even six rails (Ceulemans), it loses its steam and drifts out to touch the red.

7

Massé Shots

W. C. Fields in his famous pool skit prepares to drive his cue into
a pre-drilled hole in the slate.
(Moldenhauer Collection)

The United States once led the world in massé shooters; now they're scarcer than rack girls and ivory balls. Thousands of "No Massé Shots Allowed" signs have done their evil work. Proprietors seem to think that permitting players to raise their cues to vertical positions will lead to almost certain destruction of tables, cues, balls, and cloth. In fact, jump shots are more likely to send balls off the table, and draw shots are more likely to rip the cloth. Then too, unless you rip the cloth you can't get some proprietors to change it. If the massé shooter knows what he's doing, nobody has anything to worry about. But how can he learn what he's doing if nobody will let him practice? Massé shots are the fantasyland of billiards. Such tremendous spin can be put on the cueball that stunned spectators often suspect it is suffering from demonic possession. Sweeping curves, U-turns, jet-propelled acceleration, these are the things the massé expert deals in as he goes about his work.

As might be expected, massé action is most impressive on a brand-new cloth—the cueball skids farther before the spin takes effect. Unexpectedly, new cloth suffers less damage than an old cloth when subjected to massé shots because the slipperiness makes it harder to form a pit with a downward hit on the cueball. Too bad proprietors are at their most hysterical when the cloth is new. There is a way to duplicate new-cloth action: clean and wax the cueball; or coat it with a silicone spray, which reduces the friction between the cloth and the ball with wonderfully salubrious effects. Armorall is ideal, which Bill Hughes claims to have been the first to discover.

In both the pool and billiard sections, massé diagrams have a dashed "aiming line." The aiming line can be thought of as the intersection between the table bed and a vertical pane of glass. No matter how much you elevate your cue, keep it parallel to that imaginary pane of glass. Hoppe suggested establishing the aiming line with the cue level, then raising it to massé position. For massé shots in the world tournament that require a hard stroke, contestants use a short, fat, heavy cue. Don't risk breaking your normal cue trying the last two shots in this chapter. It was out of concern for your cue and your equipment that I didn't make the chapter longer; there are scores of magnificent shots to choose from.

American three-cushion and pool players don't often have to resort to massé shots. I hate to have to say this, but if you want to see them as they should be played, you'll have to go overseas.

Bon voyage!

Pretending to be of the opposite sex for 25 years is the most difficult trick in this book. Material remaining in Ripley's files fails to reveal whether Anderson played pool or billiards. The title he or she claimed was almost certainly self-bestowed, as her or his name appears in no list of tournament or match winners. Events for women only are a relatively recent phenomenon. To the best of my knowledge, there has never been a tournament for transvestites.

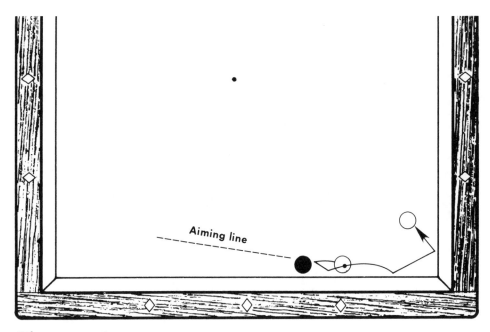

Aiming line

Short massé

This is as easy as massé shots get. Don't shoot too hard or the cueball won't have time to get back to the end rail the second time.

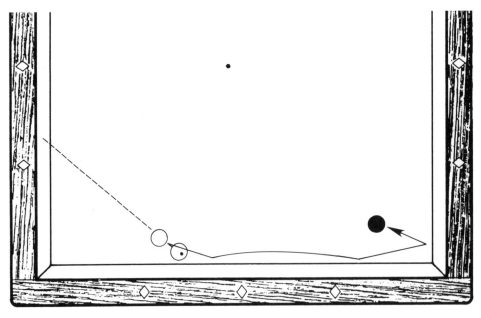

Draw massé

Action like this is also possible with a level cue. From the massé position it's much easier. Use no English, just straight backspin off the object ball.

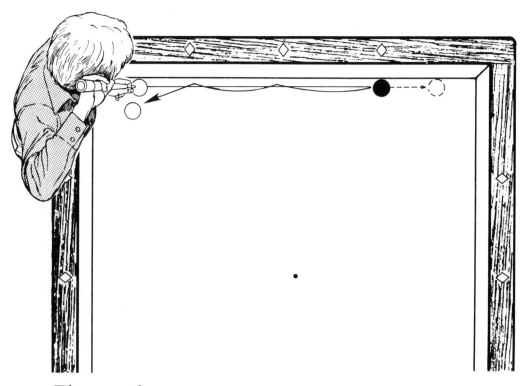

The yo-yo shot

Good for a laugh if presented properly. Announce that from the given position you will draw back from the red and hit the white without getting a kiss, which looks impossible. With a massé stroke, however, the cueball can be made to just barely touch the red before spurting backward to the white. The player in the diagram, by rights, should be Ceulemans and not me, but I couldn't afford to send an artist and a stepladder to Belgium.

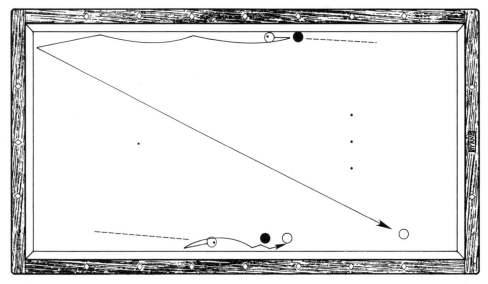

Massés long and short

Isn't the same-rail ticky at the bottom a lovely thing? Thatcher credits it to T. J. Gallagher. The big shot at the top is spectacular, but carries a difficulty rating of only five.

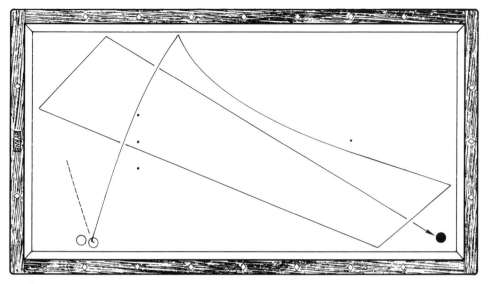

Five-rail massé

Trying to go five rails with a massé stroke is a good way to shatter your cue against the slate. The difficulty rating is eleven, which means forget it.

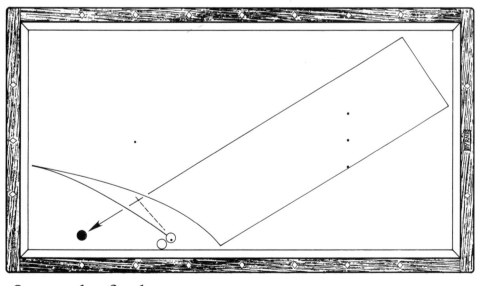

Spectacular finale

Amazing, isn't it?

Bibliography

The Noble Game of Billiards, by Captain Mingaud; translated and published by John Thurston, London, 1830. (48 pages)

This is the first English edition of Mingaud's masterwork, the first book ever written on trick shots. Forty-five of the Frenchman's best exhibition shots are diagrammed. The publisher, who was the leading billiard table manufacturer of the day, swears in a preface that he saw Mingaud execute every shot. The book is extremely rare.

The Game of Billiards, by Michael Phelan; D. Appleton and Company, New York, 1858. (268 pages)

An expansion and revision of the author's 1850 title, *Billiards Without a Master,* which was the first American book on the game. Contains twenty-eight diagrams, many showing more than one shot. Phelan was a national champion, inventor of a rubber cushion that quickly became standard, and the man who squared off snooker-style pockets to create what we now know as the pool table. His table manufacturing firm, through a series of mergers, eventually became Brunswick.

The McCleery Method of Billiard Playing, by Professor J. F. B. McCleery; author and publisher, San Francisco, 1890. (146 pages)

McCleery was a billiard-room manager in San Francisco, an instructor at the Olympic Club, an exhibition player ("clubs and residences a specialty"), and a gambler who on December 28, 1872 (he says), won thirty pounds of gold coins in Virginia City, Nevada, in a ten-and-a-half-hour game of "single-handed pin pool" against one Charles Douglass. McCleery's excellent booklet contains a hundred diagrams in two colors illustrating four hundred shots, several dozen of which qualify as trick shots. Billiards only, not pool. Rare.

Championship Billiards Old and New, by John A. Thatcher; Rand, McNally & Company, New York and Chicago, 1898. (244 pages)

Contains seventy-three drawings of three-cushion shots with brief comments. The only book (until now) that attempts to assign credit wherever possible. Charming because the author never brags about his own prowess and includes several drawings of lucky shots made by his friends. About one reverse-English, up-and-down shot he notes: "Effected at times by all the players born in Cuyahoga County, Ohio." Rare.

Tricks and Games on the Pool Table, by Fred Herrmann; Dover Publications, 1967. (96 pages)

Originally titled *Fun on the Pool Table* when it first appeared in 1902, this reprint is available from Dover Publications, 31 East Second St., Mineola, New York 11501. Mostly odd tricks, stunts, and games, but among the seventy-nine items are a dozen or so that keep showing up in other people's books — never, of course, with a nod to Fred.

Trick and Fancy Pocket Billiard Shots, anonymous; Brunswick-Balke-Collender, Chicago, 1918. (114 pages)

The author isn't named, the drawings are imprecise and sometimes flat wrong, and the descriptions are skimpy, but this collection of 105 shots is a kind of mother lode of modern trick-shot ideas, as evidenced by the repeated references I have had to make to it. Rare, unfortunately.

Trick and Fancy Shots in Pocket Billiards Made Easy, by Jimmy Caras; self-published by the author, 1948. (66 pages)

A handy booklet that has been in continuous print since its publication and is available from most billiard equipment suppliers. Contains fifty-nine of the easier trick shots, about two dozen of which appear in the previous two titles. Caras won the first of his four world titles in 1935 when he was twenty-six and still gives an occasional exhibition.

The Fabulous Mr. Ponzi, by Andrew Ponzi and Sam Edwards Levy; Alpina Publishing Co., New York, New York, 1948. (128 pages)

Mostly, a chatty, first-person account of the former world champion's career. Contains nine trick shots, including the full-fledged football shot, its first appearance in print. The book is out of print and rare.

Winning Pocket Billiards, by Willie Mosconi; Crown Publishers, Inc., New York, 1965. (142 pages)

A well-illustrated book of basics by the greatest pool player of all time, available from billiard suppliers and many bookstores. Includes diagrams of eighteen trick shots that are now in the standard repertoire.

Trick Shots for Fun and Blood, by Peter Margo and Robert Cherin; Eleven Publishing Company, Mt. Kisco, New York, 1981. (82 pages)

Thirty-four shots from the standard repertoire with brief comments. Margo gives his estimate of the odds of making each one for those interested in challenge bets. Available from dealers or from the publisher at 200 Diplomat Drive, Suite 5-G, Mt. Kisco, New York 10549. Margo is a two-time world champion and an entertaining exhibition player.

Artistic Billiards, by Bob Jewett; self-published, 1978. (96 pages)

The exact ball positions and cueball paths for the seventy-six shots used in the world artistic billiard tournament, with background information. An essential manual for anyone interested in competing nationally in this difficult form of the game. (For Jewett's address, write The American Billiard Association, 1660 Lin Lor Court, Elgin, Illinois 60120.)

Trick Shots, by Willie Jopling; self-published, 1978.

These are loose sheets, punched for binder mounting, sold in sets of half a dozen under various categories. The drawings are accurate and fully explained. (Willie Jopling is the pen name of Bill Marshall, a well-informed expert on trick shots and proposition bets.) For more information, write Jopling at P.O. Box 2215, Lynchburg, Virginia 24501.

Winning Pool and Trick Shots, by Nick Varner; self-published, 1981. (142 pages)

The 1980 world straight-pool champion devotes half of this nicely done paperback to fundamentals and half to seventy-six trick shots, many of which are not in Herrmann, Caras, or Mosconi. Order from P.O. Box 1309, Owensboro, Kentucky 42302.

The National Billiard News, a monthly newspaper published by Puhka Publishing Co., P.O. Box 487, Birmingham, Michigan 48012.

Billiards Digest, a magazine published every other month by National Bowler's Journal, Suite 2564, 875 North Michigan Avenue, Chicago, Illinois 60611.

Author's Note

Readers desiring enshrinement in future editions are invited to submit sketches of little-known or original shots to: Robert Byrne, c/o Harcourt Brace Jovanovich, Publishers, Trade Department, 1250 Sixth Avenue, San Diego, CA 92101.

Also
published by
Harcourt Brace Jovanovich

Paperbound, $12.95

"... the secret of throwing a ball and other equally vital and exciting shots and strategies are mysteries no more ... a wealth of knowledge the likes of which one could spend a lifetime searching for ... presented in a way that whets the appetite and instills an urgency to get to the table and play ... *the* definitive work on pool and billiards."
——————————————*The National Billiard News*————————————

"No doubt about it—this is the most comprehensive and finest diagrammed exposition ever devised of the 'art and science' ... techniques and strategies of pool ... and three-cushion billiards. It is, amazingly, the first guide to diagram ball movement accurately. ... Be warned: The book, which is for both novices and the very advanced, can be ruinous to family harmony. Also health: You may never see the sun again."
——————————————*Village Voice*————————————

"Thorough without being overly complex and writing in a delightful style, Byrne takes the reader from basics to most advanced shots. ..."
——————————————*Los Angeles Times*————————————

"The book I've been waiting for. The artwork, the writing, the organization, the scope ... everything is absolutely tops. A great book by the perfect author."
————Dorothy Wise, Five-Time U.S. Woman's Pool Champion ————

"Bob Byrne set out to produce the best book ever written on pool. He has succeeded. The player who owns this book will never be bored—he will always find something new to experiment with and practice on. It provides answers that many beginners spend years searching for. Even accomplished players will find something of value that can be added to their game."
————Tom Kollins, 1978 Snooker Player of the Year————
and Founder of the School for Straight Pool

"A tremendous work. It far surpasses anything else on the market, and should belong in every billiard player's library."
————Al Gilbert, Seven-Time U.S. Billiards Champion ————